PENGUIN BOOKS

Australian Slang

PENGUIN BOOKS

PENGUIN BOOKS

Published by the Penguin Group
Penguin Group (Australia)
707 Collins Street, Melbourne, Victoria 3008, Australia
(a division of Pearson Australia Group Pty Ltd)
Penguin Group (USA) Inc.
375 Hudson Street, New York, New York 10014, USA
Penguin Group (Canada)
90 Eglinton Avenue East, Suite 700, Toronto, Canada ON M4P 2Y3
(a division of Pearson Penguin Canada Inc.)
Penguin Books Ltd
80 Strand, London WC2R 0RL England
Penguin Ireland
25 St Stephen's Green, Dublin 2, Ireland
(a division of Penguin Books Ltd)
Penguin Books India Pvt Ltd
11 Community Centre, Panchsheel Park, New Delhi – 110 017, India
Penguin Group (NZ)
67 Apollo Drive, Rosedale, Auckland 0632, New Zealand
(a division of Pearson New Zealand Ltd)
Penguin Books (South Africa) (Pty) Ltd
Rosebank Office Park, Block D, 181 Jan Smuts Avenue, Parktown North,
Johannesburg, 2196, South Africa

Penguin Books Ltd, Registered Offices: 80 Strand, London, WC2R 0RL, England

First published by Penguin Group (Australia), 2008

10 9 8

Cover design by Nicholas McGuire © Penguin Group (Australia)
Text design by Claire Tice © Penguin Group (Australia)
Typeset in Berling by Post Pre-press Group, Brisbane, Queensland
Colour reproduction by Splitting Image, Clayton, Victoria
Printed in Australia by McPhersons Printing Group, Maryborough, Victoria

National Library of Australia
Cataloguing-in-Publication data:

Australian slang.

ISBN 978 0 14 300911 5

English language – Australia – Slang – Dictionaries.
Australianisms – Dictionaries.

427.994

penguin.com.au

Introduction

Australian Slang celebrates and interprets Australia's rich and vivid language. It is intended for locals as well as visitors, because many Australians have no idea quite how alien and incomprehensible their native language can be to outsiders, even to other English-speakers.

Australians do speak English, of course. But to many tourists (and even some locals), Australian English has only tenuous links with the mother tongue. Our speech is peppered with words and phrases whose arcane meanings are understood only by the initiated. It is these colourful colloquialisms that *Australian Slang* sets out to explain.

Australian slang has a few marked features. An obvious one is the habit of abbreviating words and adding 'o' or 'ie' to the end. Thus 'workers compensation' becomes 'compo', 'afternoon' becomes 'arvo' and aggressive becomes 'aggro'; while 'barbecue' becomes 'barbie', 'blowfly' becomes 'blowie' and 'budgerigar' becomes 'budgie.'

A large proportion of our slang seems to centre on a small number of topics, notably sex, alcohol (particularly beer), and intoxication – who would have thought there could be more than 30 terms for 'drunk' and 18 for 'vomit'. At the same time, the seemingly endless number of personal insults are more often than not jocular, affectionate even, rather than truly aggressive.

A range of books and dictionaries were consulted during the research process for this book, and a necessarily sceptical and discriminating eye cast over the trash and treasure trove of the internet. Language overheard being used in everyday life was also included. It is fascinating to discover the myriad and contrasting ways terms and phrases are defined and used by different people and sources. The Australian language is certainly an ever-changing and evolving entity.

Some of the terms in this book might surprise Australian residents, who never would have imagined that seemingly mundane words such as 'manchester', 'removalist' and 'fossick' could be unique to the Australian vernacular. Whether you hail from OS or from the Lucky Country itself, this book is sure to offer you new insights into the Australian language – whether it's learning a new way to insult a mate, or discovering the true meaning of 'dip your eye!'

Key

abbrev. abbreviation
acr. acronym
derog. derogatory
hist. historical
int. interjection
joc. jocular
rs rhyming slang

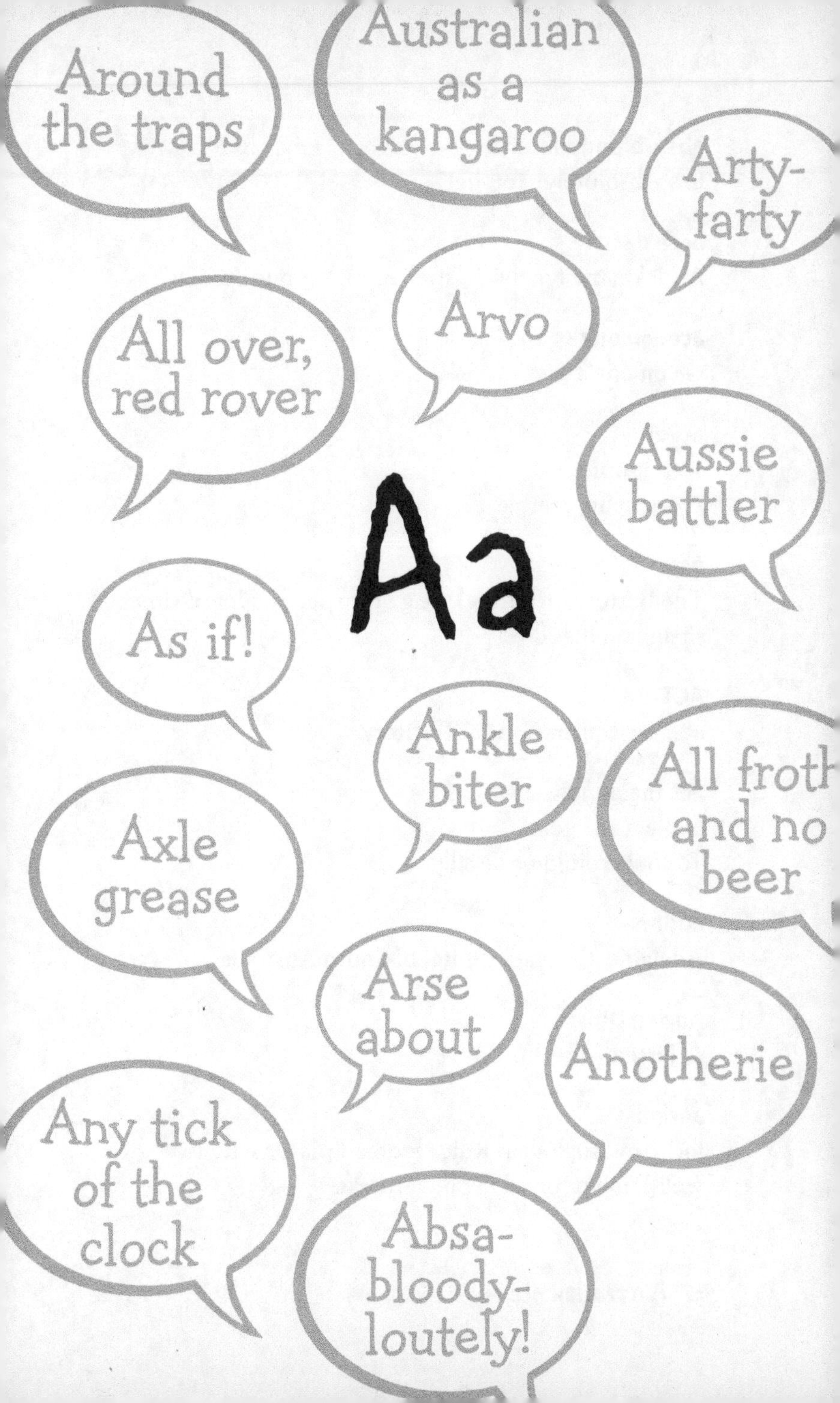
Around the traps
Australian as a kangaroo
Arty-farty
All over, red rover
Arvo
Aussie battler
Aa
As if!
Ankle biter
All froth and no beer
Axle grease
Arse about
Anotherie
Any tick of the clock
Absa-bloody-loutely!

A

absa-bloody-lutely!
int. Absolutely! You bet!

acca dacca
A nickname for the Australian rock group AC/DC.

ace, on one's
see **on one's ace**

acker
1 A pimple.
2 A playing marble.

acre
The bottom or buttocks: e.g. 'He spends a lot of times sitting on his acre.'

ACT
acr. Australian Capital Territory.

act the angora
also act the goat
To fool around or be silly.

adders
Adelaide, the state capital of South Australia.

Adrian Quist
rs Pissed (drunk).

aerialist
joc. Any Australian Rules football player who is well-known for taking high marks.

aerial ping-pong
also cross-country ballet
derog. Australian Rules football. This term is mostly used by supporters of other football codes, such as rugby and soccer.

aerogard
Any insect repellent (after the brand name).

AFL
acr. Australian Football League (the national league of Australian Rules football).

after darks
rs Sharks.

aggro
abbrev. Aggressive: e.g. 'He got really aggro and ended up punching the guy.'

aggy pipe
also ag pipe
abbrev. Agricultural (irrigation) pipe.

airy-fairy
Vague, ditzy or absent-minded.

Akubra
A brand of wide-brimmed hat made from felted rabbit fur, commonly worn by farmers and country-dwellers. Often refers to any overtly rural-style hat.

A

Albany doctor
A cold wind that blows from the Southern Ocean, affecting the coastal areas around the town of Albany in Western Australia.

alberts
hist. Rags worn on the feet by a tramp.

Al Capone
rs Telephone.

Alf
A stupid man, particularly a crude or blokey one.

alfoil
Aluminium foil (after the brand name).

Alice, the
Alice Springs, an outback town in Central Australia.

alkie
also alky; alko; alco
An alcoholic.

All Blacks, The
The name for New Zealand's national Rugby Union team.

all froth and no beer
Superficial, shallow or phoney.

all over, red rover
Complete or finished.

all over someone like a rash
Unable to keep one's hands off someone: e.g. 'At the party, she was all over him like a rash.'

all over the place like a madwoman's breakfast
Disorder or confusion; a total mess.

all piss and wind
also all wind and water
derog. Said of someone who talks rubbish, talks too much, or is rambunctious or boastful (especially when drunk).

all prick and ribs like a drover's dog
Said of someone who is skinny or undernourished.

all the go
All the rage or in fashion: e.g. 'Karaoke is all the go right now.'

all-upper
A person who bets cumulatively, or 'all up', on a number of races.

all wet
Foolish or ridiculous.

also-ran
A competitor who fails or loses in a contest or race.

amber nectar
also amber; amber fluid
Beer.

A

ambo
abbrev. An ambulance worker.

anchors
Brakes: e.g. 'Chuck out the anchors will you, I want to stop here.'

ankle-biter
A young child or toddler.

anotherie
Another; another one: e.g. 'Have you finished your beer? Can I get you anotherie?'

any tick of the clock
Any time now; before long.

Anzac
hist. A member of the Australian and New Zealand Army Corps in World War I. Nowadays often used to describe any soldier from Australia or New Zealand. (From the original acronym ANZAC.)

Anzac biscuit
A popular biscuit made from rolled oats and golden syrup.

ape-shit, go
To go crazy or lose one's temper.

Apple Isle, the
Tasmania; an *Apple Islander* is a person from that state.

apples and pears
rs Stairs.

argie-bargie or **argy-bargy**
A heated argument or arguing.

argue the toss
To question or debate a decision or order.

Aristotle
also arras; arris
rs Bottle.

around the traps
Around the place; out and about: e.g. 'I bump into him now and then around the traps.'

arse
1 The bottom or backside.
2 **derog.** An unpleasant or offensive person or thing: e.g. 'Why is he always such an arse?'

arse about or **arse around**
To clown around or dawdle.

arse into gear, get one's
To hurry up or get moving: e.g. 'Get your arse into gear, I haven't got all day!'

arse, give someone or something the
To get rid of: e.g. 'I can't wait 'til I can give this job the arse.'

arse off
also arsehole off
To leave, often quickly.

arse over tit
also A over T; AOT
Head over heels. Often used to describe an ungraceful fall: e.g. 'She tripped on the kerb and went arse over tit into the gutter.'

arse-up
A failure or botched job.

arsey
Lucky.

Arthur Murray
rs Hurry; curry (from the Arthur Murray chain of dance studios).

Arthur or Martha, not sure whether one's
Very confused or stupid.

arty-farty
derog. Pretentious or affected, specifically in relation to arts and culture.

arvo
abbrev. Afternoon: e.g. 'Shall we go shopping in the morning or in the arvo?'

ashtray on a motorbike, useful as an
see **useful as a one-legged man in an arse-kicking competition**

as if!
int. An exclamation of derision or disbelief.

as long as my arse points to the ground
Forever.

Athens of the south
Melbourne, the state capital of Victoria (due to Melbourne's large Greek population).

Aunty
The Australian Broadcasting Corporation (ABC), Australia's national public broadcaster.

Aussie
abbrev. Australian.

Aussie battler
see **battler**.

Aussieland
Australia.

Aussie Rules
Australian Rules football.

Aussie salute or **Australian salute**
see **great Australian salute**

Australian as a kangaroo
also Australian as a meat pie
Truly Australian.

Australian crawl
The freestyle or 'front crawl' swimming stroke.

Australian Rules football
The national football code, played with a pointed oval-shaped ball, with the aim of kicking the ball between the goal posts.

'ave a go, ya mug!
see **have a go, you mug!**

avo
abbrev. Avocado.

awake-up or **a wake-up**
Wary, alert or on the ball; especially in regards to potential trickery or deception: e.g. 'I'm awake-up to you, mate!'

awning over the toy shop
also veranda over the toy shop
joc. A man's beer belly.

axle grease
1 Vegemite. (Dark-brown in colour, and with a strong, salty taste, Vegemite is an enormously popular spread made from yeast extract).
2 Money.

Bald as a bandicoot
Barker's eggs
B&S ball
Belly up
Budgie smugglers
Bath-dodger
Bb
Berko
Base over apex
Bewdy
Bag of fruit
Beer o'clock
Bugger!
Beat around the bush
Best bib and tucker
Bludge

B

babbling brook
rs A cook.

backblocks
1 The outback.
2 The outer suburbs of a city.

back country
Isolated outback areas.

backing dog
A sheepdog that runs across the backs of sheep during mustering to move them along.

back of Bourke
also back of beyond
Any out-of-the-way or remote place. (Bourke is a town in New South Wales, about 800 km north-west of Sydney.)

backy or **baccy**
Tobacco.

backyard
A garden at the rear of a home.

backyard job
Something that has been done shoddily, illegally or by someone who is unqualified. Thus a *backyard mechanic* is an unqualified mechanic offering services from his garage or shed.

bad trot
see **rough trot.**

bag
To criticise or condemn: e.g. 'She's always bagging my driving.'

baggy green, the
The cap worn by members of the Australian Test cricket team.

bagman
1 **hist.** A swagman (a wanderer or itinerant worker, who carried their belongings with them in a swag).
2 **derog.** A swindler; a crook who deals with illicit money; a bookmaker.

bagman's gazette
An imaginary publication, referred to as a source of gossip or rumour.

bag of fruit
rs A suit: e.g. 'I better dig out a bag of fruit to wear to the wedding.'

bail or **bail out**
To give up or depart: e.g. 'This party's crap, let's bail.'

bail up
To corner or ambush (originally meaning to rob or hold up).

bald as a bandicoot
Completely bald.

ball and chain
derog. A chauvinistic term for wife.

ball of muscle
A very healthy, strong or energetic person.

balls and all
All-in; fervently or with great enthusiasm.

balls around
To mess about, hang around or make mischief.

balls turn into bicycle wheels and back-pedal up your arse, I hope your
joc. A curse (made famous by Barry Humphries' character Barry McKenzie).

balls-up
A fiasco, flop or debacle: e.g. 'Everything went wrong, the whole thing was a complete balls-up.'

ball-tearer
Something brilliant, amazing or thrilling: e.g. 'The footy final was a real ball-tearer.'

ball-up
The ball bounce to restart play in an Aussie Rules football game.

banana-bender
also banana-lander; banana-eater; banana-man
A person from the tropical state of Queensland, in Australia's north-east. (The term is playful rather than geographically precise, as most Australian bananas are grown in New South Wales.) *Banana City* refers to Brisbane, the state capital of Queensland.

bandicoot on a burnt ridge, to feel like a
also lonely as a bandicoot on a burnt ridge
To feel gloomy or lonely.

bandicoot
A gardening term for the act of digging down under a potato plant to remove a few potatoes, without having to dig up the whole plant: e.g. 'If you're looking for Mum, she's bandicooting in the veggie patch.'

B & S ball
A bachelors' and spinsters' ball; now often refers to any singles' ball held in the country, traditionally to give young people from far-flung areas an opportunity to get together.

bandy as a bandicoot
Extremely bandy-legged.

banged up
Pregnant.

bang in the middle
Exactly in the centre.

bang on
1 Exactly right; on the money: e.g. 'I reckon what he said in that speech was bang on.'
2 To talk incessantly or repetitiously: e.g. 'She was banging on about women's rights again.'

bangs like a dunny door in a gale
Said of someone who has sex loudly, quickly and with gusto; or of someone who is promiscuous.

bangtail muster
A muster where animals, especially cattle, are counted.

bangtails
Animals that have had their tails docked.

Banjo or **banjo**
1 The nickname of famous bush poet and author Andrew Barton 'Banjo' Paterson.
2 A shovel or spade.

barbecue stopper
A topic, statement or announcement that is exceptionally interesting, shocking or surprising – so exceptional that it would stop proceedings at a barbecue.

barbie or **barby**
also BBQ
A barbecue.

Barcoo buster
A westerly gale in Queensland. (Barcoo is a remote outback shire in far western Queensland.)

barf
To vomit.

barfly
derog. A person regularly found at a pub, often drunk.

bark at the lawn
also bark
To vomit.

barkers' eggs
Dog poo.

barmy as a bandicoot
Crazy or mad.

barney
A dispute, fight or argument.

Barnsey
A nickname for popular Australian singer Jimmy Barnes (or anyone with the surname Barnes).

barra
A barramundi. (A large fish found in northern Australia that is a popular eating fish.)

barrack
To support a team or cause: e.g. 'Who do you barrack for?' As a spectator, to encourage one's team, usually loudly.

barrel of fat
rs A hat.

Barry Crocker
rs Shocker (usually in reference to a poor performance in sport). (Barry Crocker is an Australian entertainer and actor.)

base over apex
Head over heels. Often used to describe an ungraceful fall.

bash
A party: e.g. 'We're having a bit of a bash at our place this weekend if you want to come.'

bash at, have a
To attempt or have a go at.

bastard
1 **derog.** A nasty or unpleasant person: e.g. 'I can't believe she's friends with him, he's such a bastard.'
2 A friendly term of address or endearment: e.g. 'How's it goin', ya old bastard?'
3 A sympathetic term for someone: e.g. 'His eyesight's almost gone now, poor bastard.'

bath-dodger
joc. Someone from England (from the traditional Aussie belief that the British bathe only infrequently).

battered sav
A saveloy sausage (a type of frankfurter) dipped in batter and then deep-fried.

battler
Any average, hard-working Australian, especially one who is struggling financially; most often used in the phrase *little Aussie battler*.

BBQ
see **barbie**

beak
1 Nose.
2 Magistrate or judge.
3 Male school teacher.

beanie
A tight-fitting knitted hat.

beat around the bush
To dodge the question or talk around the point: e.g. 'Stop beating around the bush and just tell me what you really think!'

beaut!
also beauty; bewdy
int. An enthusiastic expression of agreement or satisfaction. Often paired with 'bottler', as in the phrase *Bewdy, bottler!*

beddable
Sexually appealing or desirable.

beddy-byes
Bedtime (when speaking to children).

beer o'clock
Time for a beer.

bee's dick
see **by a bee's dick**

beg yours?
int. I beg your pardon? Excuse me?

bell, a
A call on the telephone: e.g. 'I'll give you a bell this arvo.'

belly up, to go
To be unsuccessful or fail: e.g. 'His gardening business went belly up in less than a year.'

belt
To strike or beat: e.g. 'I shoved him and then he belted me.'

belt up!
int. A command to be quiet or stop talking: e.g. 'Belt up right now, or else!'

bench warmer
A reserve or substitute in a sporting game who spends most or all of the game on the sidelines.

bender
A drinking spree: e.g. 'He's been on a bender since 5 o'clock Friday.'

bend the elbow
To drink a lot or get drunk.

bent as a scrub tick
Mad or stupid.

berk
An idiot or hateful person.

berko
Berserk. *To go berko* is to become crazy or out of control.

berley
1 Nonsense, capering or teasing.
2 Bait spread over the water to attract fish.

best bib and tucker
Best or most formal clothing.

betcha
A contraction of bet you: e.g. 'I betcha wish you could have had the day off work today.'

bet like the Watsons
To bet a lot of money on something.

bet on two flies crawling up a wall, would
also would bet on two flies climbing up a window
Said of a person who is obsessed with gambling. (Often used to describe Australians generally: e.g. 'Aussies love gambling so much they'd bet on two flies crawling up a wall.')

better than a poke in the eye with a burnt stick
also better than a poke in the eye with a blunt/sharp stick
An expression meaning that things aren't that bad or they could be worse.

bewdy
see **beaut**

beyond the black stump
see **black stump**

bible-basher
derog. A person who is zealously or fanatically religious.

bickie or **bikkie**
A biscuit.

biffo
A fist-fight, usually not a very serious one: e.g. 'The two footy teams had a bit of a biffo.'

big bickies or **big bikkies**
A lot of money: e.g. 'I reckon he earns big bickies.' (Bickie/bikkie is a diminutive of 'biscuit'.)

big girl's blouse
derog. An effeminate man or weakling.

big-note oneself, to
To congratulate or boast about oneself; a person who does this is a *big-noter*.

big smoke
Any city or large town.

big spit
Vomit.

big sticks
The goalposts used in Australian Rules football.

bikie
A motorbike rider, often one who is a member of a motorbike club or gang.

billabong
A waterhole, especially one that only receives water during the wet season.

billy
also billy can; jackshay; jackshea
Any container, often a tin can, used for boiling water, making tea or cooking over a fire.

billycart
1 **hist.** Any small cart used for hauling goods or belongings.
2 A child's homemade go-cart.

billy lid
rs Kid.

billyo
Quickly or at speed: e.g. 'I had to go like billyo to catch up with him.'

bindi-eye
also bindy; bindi
The small, prickly seed of the native plant *Soliva sessilis*, which can stick to the fur of animals or to one's clothes, and can be quite painful if stepped on in bare feet.

B

binge
A drinking spree.

bingle
A minor vehicle accident.

bint
derog. A woman.

biro
Any ballpoint pen (from the brand name).

bit, a
A lot, very or really: e.g. 'That's a bit harsh' or 'That bloke sure can talk a bit.'

bit average, a
Really quite bad: e.g. 'This tucker's a bit average.'

bite on, to put the
see **put the bite on**

bite your bum!
int. Get lost! Piss off! Shut up!

bitie
An insect that bites.

bitser or **bitzer**
A mixed-breed dog; a mongrel.

bizzo
abbrev. Business: e.g. 'That's none of your bizzo!'

black budgie
also butcher's canary
A blowfly (suggesting that some blowflies are as big as a budgie).

blackfella or **blackfellow**
An Aboriginal person or Torres Straight Islander. (Can be considered derogatory when used by a white person, but often used by Indigenous Australians.)

blacksmith
A bad cook.

black stump, the
An imaginary, very remote location, deemed to mark the end of civilised territory. Often used in the phrases *beyond the black stump* (meaning far into the outback or into unmapped territory) and *this side of the black stump* (anywhere nearby or known).

blasted
Very drunk.

blatting along
Travelling at high speed, usually in a vehicle: e.g. 'We were blatting along when the driver slammed the brakes on.'

blimey!
int. An exclamation of wonder or surprise.

blind or **blind drunk**
Very drunk – i.e. so drunk that vision is impaired.

blind as a bandicoot
Blind or having poor sight.

blinder
1 An outstanding performance, especially in sport.
2 A drinking spree.

blind Freddy could see that, even
An expression indicating that something is patently obvious or needs no explanation. Variations include *that wouldn't even fool blind Freddy* (that won't fool anyone).

blithered
Drunk.

block
The head: e.g. 'I'm gonna knock your block off!' (I'm very angry *or* I'm going to punch you in the head). Can also refer to one's temperament: e.g. 'He lost/did his block' (he got very angry).

bloke
1 The average laid-back, likeable Aussie guy: e.g. 'He's a great bloke, my Dad.'
2 Any Australian man: e.g. 'The blokes at work are an alright bunch.'

blokey
Very masculine, and possibly a bit rough around the edges. Blokey behaviour may include excessively watching sport or drinking beer.

blood and blister
rs Sister.

blood's worth bottling
Said of somebody who is admirable, helpful or has achieved something: e.g. 'Congratulations on the win. Your blood's worth bottling, mate!'

bloody
Often referred to as 'the great Australian adjective' due to its myriad uses: e.g. 'Bloody brilliant!', 'Bloody idiot!', 'Too bloody right!', 'Bloody hell!', 'No bloody way!'

bloody oath!
also bleedin' oath!
1 **int.** I agree! Too right! That's certainly true!
2 **int.** A general exclamation of surprise, annoyance, exasperation, etc: e.g. 'Bloody oath, I'm cold. It's freezing out here!'

blotto
Very drunk.

blow a blue dog off its chain, so windy it would
Extremely windy.

blower
A telephone: e.g. 'I better get on the blower and let everyone know what's happened.'

blowhard
A chatterbox.

blowie
A blowfly.

blow-in
A person from out of town, a newcomer, or an uninvited guest.

bludge
1 To be idle or lazy when one should be working.
2 Something simple or that doesn't require much effort: e.g. 'That exam was a bit of a bludge.'

bludger
A person who takes advantage, especially of the welfare system (as in the phrase *dole bludger*).

blue
1 An argument or brawl: e.g. 'The boys had a bit of a blue last night.'
2 A mistake or error.

bluebottle
1 Another name for the poisonous Portuguese man-of-war jellyfish.
2 A police officer.

blue heeler
A police officer (after the Australian cattle-dog breed and the colour of the police uniform).

blue-nosed wowser
see **wowser**

Bluestone College, The
hist. Melbourne's Pentridge Prison, which was surrounded by high bluestone walls. (The prison was closed in 1997 and the site has since been developed for housing, although the front gate and outer walls remain.)

bluey
1 A term of address for a red-haired person.
2 **hist.** A swag. *To hump one's bluey* means to carry one's swag. Nowadays, may refer to any form of luggage.
3 A legal summons.

Bluey and Curley
hist. Soldier characters from a popular 1940s and 50s comic strip by Alex Gurney.

blunnies
Blundstone boots. (An Australian brand of elastic-sided leather work boots. Also used to refer to any similar boot.)

BO
acr. Body odour: e.g. 'That bloke's got the worst BO!'

boardies
Board shorts.

bobby-dazzler
also dazzler
An exceptional or brilliant person, act or thing.

Bob Hope
rs Soap; dope.

bodgie
1 Of inferior quality or badly done: e.g. 'The mechanic did a really bodgie job.'
2 An insignificant or useless person. (From an Australian term of the 1950s, referring to a loutish, rock-and-roll youth.)

bogan
also bevan
derog. An uncultured, unfashionable or uncouth person.

bog catchers
Baggy tracksuit pants.

bogey or **bogie**
1 To swim.
2 A swim: e.g. 'Let's have a bogey this arvo.'
3 A glob of snot up one's nose.

bogey hole
A natural swimming hole.

bog house
An outdoor toilet.

bog in
To take part in something with gusto or fervour, especially eating.

boiler
derog. An unattractive or older woman. (Originally used to describe chickens that were too old and scrawny to roast.)

boilover
A situation in which an unknown competitor defeats the favourite; any unexpected result or outcome. Often used in horseracing.

boil the billy
Put the kettle on, usually to make a cup of tea.

boil-up
An argument or fight.

bollocks!
1 **int.** Rubbish! Nonsense! e.g. 'Be quiet, you're talking bollocks!'
2 Testicles: e.g. 'He kicked me right in the bollocks.'

bollocky, in the
Naked; in the nude.

bolt
1 To depart suddenly and unexpectedly: e.g. 'Her bloke did a bolt and didn't leave her two bob.'
2 *To bolt food down* is to eat it very quickly.

bomb
1 Any old, rusty or broken-down car.
2 To fail.

bombed
Drunk.

bombo
Cheap wine, usually of poor quality.

bombora
also bommie; bommy
A hidden reef or rocky area, which causes large waves to form. Also, especially in surfing, the wave formed by a such a feature.

Bondi cigar
A piece of human faeces floating in the ocean. (In the past there was a sewage outlet near Sydney's famous Bondi beach.)

Bondi tram
see **shoot through like a Bondi tram**

bonehead
A foolish or stupid person.

bonkers
Mad, crazy or extremely angry: e.g. 'Mum went bonkers when I broke the vase.'

bonza or **bonzer**
An adjective expressing delight or approval: e.g. 'That was a bonzer barbie.'

booay
An isolated or remote outback area.

boofhead
A dim-witted or foolish person. (A generally light-hearted insult.)

bookie
A bookmaker.

boomer
A male kangaroo.

boomerang
1 An Aboriginal throwing stick used for hunting animals and designed to return to the thrower.
2 Anything that returns, such as a cheque that bounces.

booze
Alcohol.

booze artist
A person who drinks a lot.

booze bus
A mobile police vehicle used to test the blood-alcohol content of drivers.

boozed
Drunk.

boozer
A place where one goes to drink, usually a pub: e.g. 'I'm just off to the boozer.'

booze-up
A drinking session or party.

bo-peep
1 A sneaky look.
2 rs A sleep.

bored shitless
Very bored.

boring as batshit
Very boring.

born in a tent, were you
A question addressed to someone who leaves the door open.

boss cocky
The boss; the person in charge or giving the orders.

bot
1 To borrow or cadge, especially money.
2 A person who consistently sponges off others.

botch
also botch up
To make a mess of or spoil something: e.g. 'My mechanic botched the repair job on my car. Now it won't even start.'

bottie
abbrev. A bottom.

bottler!
int. An expression of enthusiasm, approval or admiration. Often paired with 'bewdy', as in the phrase *Bewdy, bottler!*

bottle shop
also bottle-o
A liquor store.

bottom-of-the-harbour scheme
A tax-dodge or tax-avoidance scheme. (After a well-known tax-avoidance scheme common in the 1970s, where in-debt companies were stripped of their assets and then hidden – i.e. 'sent to the bottom of the harbour' – without paying their tax debts.)

bottoms up!
int. Cheers!

bower bird
1 A person who collects junk or trivial objects.
2 A petty thief.
(After the male of an Australian bird species, which collects bright, shiny objects to decorate its nest or 'bower'.)

bowser
A petrol pump.

box of birds, like a
Happy or chirpy: e.g. 'She's been like a box of birds since her promotion.'

boys in blue
Police officers (usually refers to the police in general): e.g. 'The boys in blue turned up to keep the crowd under control.'

Bradbury, do a
To have an unusual, lucky or undeserved win or success. (After ice-skater Steven Bradbury, who won a gold medal in the men's short track 1000 metres event at the 2002 Winter Olympic Games after all of his competitors crashed on the final corner.)

Brahms and Liszt
rs Pissed.

brasco
also braska
A toilet.

brassed, to be
To be tricked or deceived.

brass monkey weather
Extremely cold weather conditions.
see also **cold enough to freeze the balls off a brass monkey**

brass razoo, not have a
also not have a cracker; not have a brass rahzoo
To have no money or spare cash. *Not worth a brass razoo* means not worth anything.

break open a coldie
also crack a tinnie
To open a beer.

breakers, shoot the
see **shoot the breakers**

breezer
A fart.

brekkie or **brekky**
Breakfast.

breville
A toasted sandwich or toasted sandwich maker (after the brand name of a toasted sandwich maker).

brew
A cup or pot of tea: e.g. 'Make a brew would you, love?'

brickfielder
A dry wind that carries a lot of dust or sand, often hot and blowing from the desert.

brickie
abbrev. A bricklayer.

brickie's cleavage
see **builder's crack**

brick short of a load, a
also a brick short of a wall
Said of a stupid or dim-witted person.

brick venereal
A brick veneer house.

brigalow
A species of Australian acacia tree; also the areas where such trees grow.

bright-eyed and bushy-tailed
Fit, in good health and rearing to go.

Brisbanite
A person from Brisbane, the state capital of Queensland.

Brissie or **Brizzie**
Brisbane.

Bris-Vegas
joc. Brisbane (referring to the common opinion that Brisbane is a dull city).

brits
also britts; Jimmy Brits; jimmies
rs Shits. *To have the brits* is to be mad or angry and *to have the brits up* is to be scared or startled.

broke for, to be
In need of or short of something: e.g. 'I'm broke for a place to stay.'

brolly
Umbrella.

Brownlow Medal, the
also the Brownlow
A trophy awarded each year to the AFL player voted best and fairest of the season.

Bruce
Any typical Australian bloke.

brumby
A wild horse.

brummy
Inexpensive; of poor or inferior quality.

brunch
A meal taken mid-morning as a substitution for breakfast and lunch.

BS
abbrev. Bullshit.

bub
Baby: e.g. 'Could you just hold the bub for a sec while I run her a bath?'

bubbler
A drinking fountain.

bubbly or **bubbles**
Sparkling wine or champagne.

buck
A dollar: e.g. 'He worked at the farm to earn a quick buck.'

B

bucker
A horse that bucks.

Buckley's chance
also Buckley's
A very slim chance, or no chance at all: e.g. 'He's got Buckley's chance of winning.' (After William Buckley, a convict who escaped and survived against the odds.)

bucks' night
also stag night
A celebration attended by a groom and his male friends before his wedding day – traditionally a rowdy night of excessive drinking and debauched behaviour.

buck up
To cheer up.

budgie
Budgerigar. (A small Australian parrot often kept as a pet.)

budgie smugglers
also cock jocks; peeny pointers; lolly bag
joc. Speedos (a tight-fitting style of men's bathers).

buggalugs or **buggerlugs**
1 Whatsisname.
2 A usually affectionate term of address for someone who is a bit silly or annoying.

bugger

1 An expression of annoyance or anger: e.g. 'Bugger! I've bogged the bloody ute again!'
2 Any man: e.g. 'He's a mad old bugger.'
3 A nasty or unpleasant person.
4 An annoyance or problem: e.g. 'Getting the kids to go to bed is a real bugger.'

bugger about

also bugger around
To clown around, act foolishly or dawdle: e.g. 'Stop buggering about and get back to work.'

bugger-all

Nothing or a very small amount: e.g. 'He knows bugger-all about horseracing.'

buggered

1 Tired or worn out. 'I'm always buggered by the end of my shift at work.'
2 Broken or ruined: e.g. 'He buggered our lawnmower by running over the hose.'

Bugger me dead!

int. An expression of surprise or amazement.

bugger off!

1 **int.** Piss off!
2 To depart or go away: e.g. 'He buggered off home after lunch.'

buggery

1 An imaginary far-off place. Thus *Go to buggery!* means 'Get lost!' If something has *gone to buggery* it has declined in quality or got worse: e.g. 'That restaurant's gone to buggery since the new chef started.'

2 A lot: e.g. 'I had to work like buggery to get it all done in time.'

bugle

Nose. Thus *to blow the bugle* means to blow one's nose.

bug off!

int. Piss off! Get lost!

builder's crack

also brickie's cleavage

The cleft of the buttocks, exposed above the waist of one's pants; deemed to be an omnipresent spectacle at building sites.

built like a brick shithouse

A term for someone who is particularly large, strong or stocky.

Bullamakanka

Any remote, far-away or alien place; a mythical outback town.

bullshit

also bull; bulldust; bullswool; baloney

1 Untrue, false or exaggerated talk: e.g. 'That's a load of bull and you know it.'

2 **int.** An expression of disbelief or anger: e.g. 'Bullshit! You're making it up!'

bum floss
G-string underwear (the equivalent of a US thong).

bum full of Smarties, silly as a
see **silly as a hatful of worms**

bum nut
An egg.

bum sniffers
derog. Rugby League players.

bundy
abbrev. Bundaberg rum (an Australian brand of rum): e.g. 'I'll have a bundy and coke, thanks.'

bung
1 To put or place, especially carelessly: e.g. 'Bung another snag on the barbie.'
2 Broken or impaired: e.g. 'The left one's my bung eye.'

bung it on
To put on a show, be excessive or pretentious.

bunyip
A fearsome creature of Aboriginal mythology, thought to inhabit billabongs.

bunyip aristocracy
hist./derog. Australians who consider themselves to be upper class, noble or refined; or who act in a snobbish or imperious way. (Coined in the 1850s when various colonial parliaments tried to establish titled aristocracy.)

burl, give it a
also give it a whirl
To attempt or try something: e.g. 'Sure, I'll give it a burl.'

burn off
To burn rubbish in a bonfire, or to burn scrub to clear land.

bush
1 Australian forest or scrubland.
2 *The bush* is anywhere outside of or beyond urban settlements.

bush ballad
A poem depicting experiences of life in the Australian bush.

bush-bash
To make a path through dense native bushland; to go off the marked track.

Bush Capital, the
Canberra, the capital city of Australia. (So-called because Canberra was built in a rural area, halfway between Melbourne and Sydney.)

bush carpenter
An amateurish carpenter, especially one who is unqualified or untrained.

bush cattle
Cattle that roam in unfenced bushland.

bush chook
An emu.

bush dance
A dance conducted in traditional bush fashion, with country music and dancing.

bushed
1 Very tired.
2 Lost or confused.

bushfire
A fire in bushland.

bushfire blond
A red-haired person.

bushie
1 A person who lives in a rural or outback area; a bushman.
2 Someone who is unsophisticated.

bush lawyer
Someone with no formal legal training who offers legal advice, opinion or argument.

bushman
A person with enough knowledge of the Australian bush to be able to survive there.

bushman's breakfast
A breakfast consisting of not much.

bushman's alarm
also bushman's clock; settler's clock
A kookaburra (an Australian bird with a loud, laughter-like call).

bush medicine
Traditional Aboriginal remedies and treatments for illness.

bush mile
An approximate, and often underestimated, calculation of a mile. (The Aussie variation of a 'country mile'.)

bush pig
derog. An ugly or unpleasant woman.

bushranger
hist. An outlaw who lived in the bush and robbed travellers and settlers.

bush tea
Tea brewed in a billy over a camp fire.

bush telegraph
also bush telegram
An unofficial network used for passing news and gossip through the community; the grapevine.

bush telly
1 The night sky. (Looking at the stars is one of the few forms of entertainment when camping in the bush.)
2 The camp fire. (For the same reason as above.)

bush tucker
1 Food gathered from native Australian plants and animals in the bush.
2 Traditional Aboriginal food.

bushwalk
A recreational hike or trek through the bush. *Bushwalking* is the activity itself.

Bush Week
1 **hist.** An event during which country folk came to the city.
2 Often used in the expression *What do you think this is, Bush Week?*, meaning 'Do you think I'm stupid?'

bushwhacked or **bushwacked**
1 Very tired or completely exhausted.
2 Surprised or astonished.

bushwhacker
An unrefined person who lives in the bush or a rural area.

busy as a blue-arsed fly
also busy as a cat burying shit; busy as a one-legged man in an arse-kicking competition
Very busy.

butcher's canary
see **black budgie.**

butcher's hook
also butchers
rs A look.

by a bee's dick
By an extremely small margin: e.g. 'They won the game, but only by a bee's dick.'

BYO
acr. Bring your own. Indicates a restaurant where diners may bring their own alcohol. Also used more generally to specify what one should bring to a social gathering or event: e.g. BYO sunscreen and chair. *BYOG* means BYO grog.

Cc
Carry on like a pork chop
Cheese and kisses
Carpet grub
Choof off
The Centre
Cooee!
Cackle-berry
Cheap and cheerful
Crack a tinnie
Come a cropper
Cunning as a dunny rat
Cattle duffer
Chuck a sickie

C

cab sav
Cabernet sauvignon wine.

cack-handed
1 Left-handed.
2 Clumsy.

cack oneself, to
To laugh heartily: e.g. 'When I told her the joke she cacked herself.'

cackleberry
An egg.

cactus
Broken or useless: e.g. 'The microwave's cactus.'

Cadbury, a
joc. A person who gets drunk from very few drinks, or even from just 'a glass and a half'. (After Cadbury's slogan, which boasts that there's 'a glass and a half of full-cream dairy milk' in every block of their chocolate.)

cakehole
Mouth: e.g. 'Shut your cakehole!'

call a spade a bloody shovel
The Aussie version of 'call a spade a spade.'

call Ralph
also call Ruth
To vomit.

Canberran
A person from Canberra, Australia's capital city.

cane
1 To defeat an opponent in competition, often by a wide margin: e.g. 'We caned them in the finals!'
2 To attack or beat.

Captain Cook
rs A look. (Captain James Cook was the first European to map the coastline of Australia.)

cardie
abbrev. Cardigan.

cark it
also kark it
To die or break: e.g. 'The bloody tractor's gone and carked it.'

c'arn! or **carn!**
int. Come on! Used to encourage one's team when barracking: e.g. 'C'arn the Roos/Pies/Crows!'

carpet grub
Young child or baby.

carry Matilda
also carry a Matilda
hist. To carry a swag (a roll of personal belongings and bedding).

carry on like a pork chop
To make a fuss, overreact or complain: e.g. 'Stop carrying on like a pork chop and go and do your homework.'

cask wine
also goon
Wine stored in an airtight bag which is enclosed in a cardboard box and dispensed through a plastic tap (believed to have been developed by a winemaker in South Australia).

cast-for-age
(of a sheep, horse or cow) Too old for breeding.

catch a fly in a country dunny, couldn't
Said of a stupid or useless person.

cattle duffer
Cattle thief. *Cattle duffing* is the act of stealing cattle.

cattle station
A farm where cattle are bred for their meat.

caulie
abbrev. Cauliflower.

Centre, The
The arid desert centre of Australia, especially the southern part of the Northern Territory, of which Alice Springs is the largest settlement. Often *The Red Centre*.

chalkie
A school teacher.

champers
Champagne or sparkling wine.

chardy
Chardonnay wine.

charge like a wounded bull
also charge like the light brigade
To charge too much, or set very high or inflated prices. 'I never go to that barber, he charges like a wounded bull.'

cheap and cheerful
Something reasonably priced that is nonetheless perfectly satisfactory.

cheap and nasty
Inexpensive and of poor quality.

cheap as chips
Very inexpensive.

cheapie
Something inexpensive: e.g. 'This bottle of wine's not bad for a cheapie.'

checkout chick
A woman who works at the cash register in a supermarket.

cheer chaser
derog. A sycophantic person, especially one seeking overt or public praise.

cheerio
1 Goodbye: e.g. 'We'll be off then. Cheerio!'
2 Hello or regards: e.g. 'Give a cheerio to your missus from us.'

cheese and kisses
rs Missus (wife).

chew and spew
joc. A fast-food restaurant or cafe.

chewie
Chewing gum.

chewie on your boot!
int. A shout by spectators at an Aussie Rules football match, intended to distract a player attempting to kick a goal.

chiack or **chiak**
To make fun of, tease, banter or fool about.

chillax
Chill out and relax: e.g. 'Let's just chillax tonight after work.'

china plate
also china
rs Mate.

chippie
A carpenter.

chips
1 Packaged potato chips or crisps.
2 Hot chips or French fries.

chockers
Very full (contraction of 'chock-full' or 'chock-a-block'): e.g. 'The train was chockers.'

chockies
abbrev. Chocolates.

choice
Excellent or first-rate.

choke a brown dog, would
also would kill a brown dog
Very bad, especially of food: e.g. 'This pie is so bad it'd choke a brown dog.'

choof off
To depart or go: e.g. 'I guess I better choof off soon.'

chook
1 A chicken; chicken meat.
2 **derog.** A woman, especially an old or ugly one: e.g. 'She's a grumpy old chook.'

chook chaser
derog. A small motorcycle, especially a dirt bike, or a person who rides such a bike.

chook house
A chicken house or shed.

chooks turn into emus and kick your dunny down, I hope all your
also I hope all your chooks turn into emus and kick your house down
joc. A curse.

chop chop!
int. Be quick! Come on, hurry it up!

Chrissie or **Chrissy**
Christmas.

Christmas on a stick
Something wonderful or magnificent: e.g. 'What do you think you are, Christmas on a stick?'

chrome dome
A man with a bald head.

chuck
1 Vomit.
2 To throw, put or do: e.g. 'Chuck us a tinnie, will you mate?'
see also **chuck a fit; chuck a sickie; chuck it in**

chuck a fit
also chuck a spaz; chuck a wobbly
To throw a tantrum or become very angry.

chuck a sickie
To take sick leave, especially dishonestly.

chuck it in
To give up on an attempt or quit: e.g. 'As for my job, I've chucked it in. The pay was terrible.'

chug-a-lug
To drink an alcoholic beverage quickly or all in one go; to skol.

chunder
Vomit.

chuttie or **chutty**
Chewing gum.

City of Churches
Adelaide, the state capital of South Australia.

city slicker
A person who lives in an urban area.

clag the bag
To die: e.g. 'I can't believe he clagged the bag just a week before his eightieth birthday.'

clagged out
1 Broken or not working: e.g. 'The bus clagged out halfway there.'
2 Tired or worn out.

clanger
A gaff or blunder; a conversation stopper.

claret
Blood (after the type of wine).

claytons
A substitute or imitation (after a brand of non-alcoholic drink).

clever, not too
Not very well or healthy.

click
A kilometre: e.g. 'My mate lives about 15 clicks from here.'

clodhoppers
1 Feet, especially big ones.
2 A *clodhopper* is a clumsy person.

close to the knuckle
Offensive, vulgar or improper: e.g. 'That was a bit close to the knuckle.'

clucky
A person who feels maternal and keen to have children, or who is assessed by others to be so.

cluey
Intelligent or knowledgeable.

Coathanger, the
The Sydney Harbour Bridge (after its shape).

cobber
1 A friend. *To cobber up* means to become friends.
2 An informal term of address: e.g. 'G'day, cobber!'

cobblers
1 Nonsense: e.g. 'That's a load of old cobblers!'
2 **rs** Balls (testicles). (A contraction of cobblers awls.)

cockatoo
A lookout, originally one used during illegal games of two-up (after the native parrot of that name.)

cock jocks
see **budgie smugglers**

cocky
1 A farmer, especially one with only a small amount of land.
2 **abbrev.** A cockatoo. (An Australian species of parrot that is white with a golden crest.)

codswallop
Rubbish or nonsense.

coit
see **quoit**

cold as a witch's tit
Extremely cold.

cold enough to freeze the balls off a brass monkey
also brass monkey weather
Extremely cold.

coldie
A cold beer.

come a cropper
also come a gutser
1 To have a bad fall or accident.
2 To make a mistake or fail at something.

come again?
int. Excuse me? Pardon? Could you say that again?

come down in the last shower, I didn't
I'm not stupid/naive/gullible.

come good
1 To recover, improve or be put right: e.g. 'I was feeling a bit sick earlier, but I've come good.'
2 To produce something, particularly in response to a request or promise: e.g. 'My boss came good with that raise he'd promised.'

come in on the grouter, to
To exploit or gain an advantage, particularly a financial one and often an unfair one. (Originally used in the gambling game of two-up.)

come in spinner!
int. A phrase used to suggest that someone has been tricked or deceived. (Originally used in the gambling game of two-up as a call for the coins to be tossed by the 'spinner'.)

come on to
To chat up or flirt with: e.g. 'He was coming on to me, but I told him where to go.'

comic cuts
rs Guts.

compo
abbrev. Worker's Compensation.

conk
Nose.

conk out
To break down or stop working.

convo
abbrev. Conversation.

cooee!
int. A loud and often echoing cry used to attract attention or call for help in the bush. *Within cooee* means nearby or not far away, i.e. within hearing distance.

Coolgardie safe
hist. A wooden box draped with wet sacking, used as a crude refrigerator. (Named after the small mining town of Coolgardie in Western Australia where it was invented.)

coot
An affectionate term of address: e.g. 'He's not a bad old coot.'

cop or **copper**
A police officer.

cop a serve
To be scolded or berated by someone.

cop shop
A police station.

corker
Something excellent, striking or surprising: e.g. 'What a corker!'

Corner Country
The remote area where the state borders of South Australia, Queensland and New South Wales meet. (The actual meeting point is known as Cameron Corner.)

cossie or **cozzie**
A swimming costume.

cot
A bed (not necessarily a child's bed).

cot-case
A person who is very ill, very tired or very drunk, and who is (or should be) confined to bed.

couldn't work in an iron lung
see **work in an iron lung**

couple of meat pies short of a grand final
see **meat pies short of a grand final**

cove
1 **hist.** The boss or manager of a station or shop.
2 A man.

cow
1 Disagreeable or unwelcome: e.g. 'What a cow of a morning it's been.'
2 An ugly, offensive or nasty woman.

cow cocky
A cattle farmer.

crack a fat
To get an erection.

crack a tinnie
also break open a coldie
To open a beer.

cracker, not worth a
Worthless.

crack hardy or **crack hearty**
To suffer or tolerate with patience or courage; to put on a brave face.

crack on to
To hit on or chat up: e.g. 'He tried cracking on to me, but I told him I have a boyfriend.'

crack the whip
To push someone to work or perform a task more quickly: e.g. 'My boss was really cracking the whip today.'

crap
Bad or terrible: e.g. 'I had such a crap day at work; everything went wrong!'

crap on
To talk too much, in an irritating or long-winded way: e.g. 'Stop crapping on.'

crapper
A toilet.

crash-hot
Very good, excellent or well. Often used in the negative: e.g. 'I'm not feeling all that crash-hot today.'

crawler
A sycophant or flatterer.

crikey!
also crikes; cripes
int. An exclamation of surprise or wonder.

crim
abbrev. A criminal.

croc
abbrev. A crocodile.

crook
1 Ill or sick: e.g. 'I won't be coming in to work today; I feel really crook.'
2 *To go crook at/on someone* means to berate or get angry at someone.
3 Unreliable or of dubious quality.

crook as Rookwood
Very ill or dying. (Rookwood is a cemetery in Sydney.)

crooked as a dog's hind leg
Said of a dishonest person or criminal.

cross-country ballet
see **aerial ping-pong**

cross-country wrestling
derog. Rugby League. Often used by supporters of Aussie Rules football; the term reflects the amount of tackling and tussling that goes on in the sport.

crow-eater
A person from South Australia (from the Australian Rules football team of that state, the Adelaide Crows).

crownie
abbrev. Crown Lager (a popular Australian beer).

crown jewels
also family jewels
The male genitals: e.g. 'The bastard kicked me right in the crown jewels.'

cruet
Head.

crumblies
Elderly people, often one's parents.

crust, a
A source of income or livelihood: e.g. 'What do you do for a crust?'

cry Ruth
To vomit.

cubby house
also cubby
A children's playhouse, usually located outdoors.

cultural cringe
The collective inferiority complex, whereby Aussie culture is seen to be inferior to that of other countries, particularly England.

cunning as a dunny rat
also cunning as a shithouse rat
Extremely cunning (the Aussie version of 'cunning as a fox').

Cup Day
A public holiday in Melbourne in honour of the annual Melbourne Cup horserace.

cup of chino
also cuppa chino
A deliberate mispronunciation of cappuccino.

cup of tea, a Bex and a good lie down
see **nice cup of tea, a Bex and a good lie down**

cuppa
A cup of tea: e.g. 'Won't you stay for a cuppa?'

curly
A nickname for a bald man.

cushy
Easy and/or well-paid: e.g. 'He's got such a cushy job.'

cut, to be
To be really annoyed or angry: e.g. 'I was cut when I realised they'd ripped me off.'

cut one up, to
To amuse or make one laugh: e.g. 'This show really cuts me up.'

Dole bludger
Down Under
Don't come the raw prawn!
Drop one's lunch
Drongo
Dd
Dinkum oil
Drink with the flies
Dingbat
Dead horse
A dingo's breakfast
Drive the porcelain bus
Dad and Dave
Drunk as a piss-ant
Dag

dack

To pull someone's pants down: e.g. 'She dacked him right in front of everyone!'

Dad and Dave

rs A shave. (Dad and Dave were popular fictional characters created by Australian author Arthur Hoey Davis, aka Steele Rudd.)

dag

A person who dresses or behaves in an unfashionable manner; an eccentric or odd person. Such a person can be said to be *daggy*. (Dags are also the tufts of wool around a sheep's bottom, which are commonly covered in excrement.)

daks

Trousers or pants.

dam

A man-made body of water, especially one built on a farm: e.g. 'We've had so little rain, the dam in the top paddock's bone dry.'

damage

The charge or cost: e.g. 'So what's the damage for this meal?'

damper

Simple unleavened bread, usually baked in the coals of a camp fire.

D and M
abbrev. Deep and meaningful (referring to an apparently serious or emotional conversation): e.g. 'Don't interrupt them, they're having a D and M about her lousy bloke.'

dangle a line
Go fishing.

darl
abbrev. Darling. Used to address any woman, whether friend, acquaintance or stranger: e.g. 'Excuse us, darl, could you tell me what aisle the eggs are in?'

dart
A cigarette.

Darwinian
also Darwinite
A person from Darwin, the capital of the Northern Territory.

date
An anus (after the fruit.)

dazzler
see **bobby-dazzler**

dead centre
also dead heart
The arid desert areas of central Australia.

deadhead
derog. A stupid, boring or useless person.

D

dead horse
rs Sauce, especially tomato sauce.

dead ringer
A person or thing that is almost identical to another.

dead set
1 True or genuine: e.g. 'I'm not lying, it's dead set!'
2 Truthfully or genuinely: e.g. 'Dead set, it wasn't me.'

deadshit
An offensive, nasty or otherwise detestable person.

death adders in one's pocket, to have
To be miserly or stingy with money.

decko or **dekko**
A look: e.g. 'Take a decko at that sports car!'

delish
abbrev. Delicious.

demo
abbrev. Demonstration.

dero or **derro**
A tramp or homeless person. (An abbreviation of derelict.)

dice
To get rid of or throw away: e.g. 'Dice that carton of milk, it's gone off.'

dick
also dickhead
derog. An idiot, especially a male: e.g. 'That guy is such a dick, I can't stand him.'

dickless Tracy
derog. A policewoman.

die in the arse
To fail or fall short, often before completion: e.g. 'That idea died in the arse pretty quickly.'

diddle
To con or deceive.

digger
1 A gold miner.
2 An Australian or New Zealand soldier, especially one who served in World War I.
3 A friendly term of address, similar to 'mate.'

dill
also dillpot
A foolish or silly person: e.g. 'You can be such a dill sometimes.'

dillybag
A small carry bag. (Originally a woven bag used by Indigenous Australians.)

dingbat
An odd, silly or eccentric person.

dingo
derog. A cheat, coward or despicable person. *To dingo on someone* means to deceive or betray someone. (From the type of wild dog domesticated by Indigenous Australians.)

dingo's breakfast, a
joc. A piss, a scratch and a good sniff around; a minimal breakfast.

dingo did it, a
An expression used to avoid taking the blame for something. (From a notorious murder case of the 1980s, in which Lindy Chamberlain was convicted of killing her baby daughter, despite her claims that a dingo had taken the child. She was later exonerated.)

dingo fence
see **dog fence**

dink or **double-dink**
To carry a passenger on one's bicycle.

dinkum
also dinky-di
Genuine, true or truthful. Often used in the expression *fair dinkum*.

dinkum oil
The genuine truth.

dip south, to
To search in one's pocket for money.

dipstick
An idiot or no-hoper.

dip your left eye in hot cocky cack!
also dip your left eye in hot cocky shit!; dip your eye!
1 **int.** An exclamation of disdain or dismissal (coined in the 1972 film *The Adventures of Barry McKenzie*).
2 **int.** Get lost! Piss off!

dirty big
Very big: e.g. 'That's a dirty big dog.'

dirty on, be
To be angry or annoyed with.

divvy up
To divide up or share out.

divvy van
A police van.

dob in or **dob on**
To report someone's misbehaviour or tell tales on a person. Someone who dobs is labelled a *dobber*.

doco
abbrev. A documentary film.

docket
Receipt: e.g. 'Make sure you keep the docket in case you need to exchange it.'

dodger
Food or bread.

dog
derog. An ugly woman.

dog and bone
rs Phone.

dog fence, the
also the dingo fence
A 10 000 km fence stretching from south-eastern Queensland to south-western South Australia. Built in the late 19th century, it is still used (generally unsuccessfully) to keep dingos from entering south-eastern Australia.

dogs, the
Greyhound racing.

dog's breakfast, a
A confused or messy thing, person or situation: e.g. 'You look like a dog's breakfast today!'

dog's eye
rs Meat pie.

doh ray me
rs Dough (money): e.g. 'Could you lend me a bit of the doh ray me?'

dole, the
Unemployment or welfare benefits paid by the government.

dole bludger
derog. A person who takes advantage of the government welfare system.

domestic, a
A domestic dispute or fight: e.g. 'The neighbours were having a bit of a domestic last night.'

Don, the
Sir Donald Bradman, perhaps the most famous and legendary cricketer in Australian sporting history.

done like a dinner
1 Completed or finished.
2 Defeated in a competition.

done up like a sore toe
Dressed up or overdressed.

dong
1 To hit.
2 Penis. (*also* donger)

donkey vote
In a political ballot, a vote that has deliberately been cast to be invalid, usually by inserting numbers on the voting slip in order, from the top to the bottom.

Dons, the
A nickname for the Essendon AFL team.

don't do anything you couldn't eat!
An Aussie variation on 'Don't bite off more than you can chew!'

don't come the raw prawn (with me)
A scornful response meaning 'Don't try to fool me.'

don't piss down my back and tell me it's raining
joc. Don't lie to me or try to pull the wool over my eyes.

don't wake it up
Leave it be. An Australian variation on 'Let sleeping dogs lie.'

doona
Any duvet or continental quilt (after the brand name).

doover
also dooverlackie; doodad
Something you can't remember or think of a name for: e.g. 'Pass me that dooverlackie will you?'

doozey
Something excellent, wonderful or exceptional.

dork
A nerdy or unfashionable person.

Dorothy Dixer, a
A question asked in such a way as to solicit a particular answer, particularly in a parliamentary setting; a question with an obvious answer. (After American journalist Dorothy Dix, who purportedly made up questions for her own advice column so that she could write more interesting answers.)

dosh
Money, particularly cash.

dot
The bottom or backside.

down the tube
also down the gurgler
1 Lost or failed: e.g. 'That business has gone down the tube.'
2 *To send something/someone down the tube* means to sack or dismiss it/them.

Down Under
Australia; in Australia: e.g. 'It's been eight years since I came to live Down Under.'

downy bird
A shrewd or canny person: e.g. 'Luckily for me, my accountant is a downy bird.'

drack
derog. Unattractive or dishevelled.

drag the chain
To dally or fall behind in an activity, especially work: e.g. 'Stop dragging the chain and finish digging that hole!'

drain the dragon
also drain the main vein; drain the potatoes
(of a man) To urinate.

dreaming, the
also the dreamtime
The Indigenous Australian mythology of how the world came into being.

drink with the flies
To drink by oneself.

drive the porcelain bus
To vomit into the toilet (i.e. while holding onto the bowl with both hands, as one might hold a steering wheel).

drongo
An idiotic, foolish or stupid person. (After a 1920s racehorse that didn't win a single race during its career.)

droob
A geeky, boring or slow person.

drop bear
An imaginary, vicious and carnivorous relative of the koala that drops from the trees onto its unsuspecting victims. (Aussies love to scare tourists and newcomers with this story.)

dropkick
derog. A useless or stupid person, or a no-hoper.

drop one's bundle
To fall apart emotionally or give up, usually out of despair or because of failure.

drop one's lunch
To pass wind.

drover
also overlander
A person who drives cattle, usually over long distances.

drover's dog
A person who lets themselves get pushed around or works hard for poor wages; a nobody.
see also **all prick and ribs like a drover's dog; work like a drover's dog**

drown some worms, go
Go fishing.

drum, the
The truth, information or good counsel: e.g. 'He gave me the drum.'

drunk as a lord
also drunk as a skunk; drunk as Chloe
Very drunk.

drunk as a piss-ant
Extremely drunk.
see also **game as a piss-ant; piss-ant around.**

dry, the
The hot rainless season in Australia's central and northern regions, generally considered to be from May to September. (As opposed to the wet.)

dry as a dead dingo's donger
also dry as a nun's nasty; dry as a Pom's towel
Very thirsty or dry.

dry old stick
A friendly term for an elderly person.

ducks and drakes
rs The shakes (delirium tremens).

duck's guts, the
Something wonderful or excellent: e.g. 'That movie was the duck's guts.'

duds
Men's trousers.

duffer
A fairly inoffensive, even affectionate, term for a daft or dim person: e.g. 'Pick yourself up you silly duffer.'

Dunlop overcoat
A condom. (Dunlop is a company that manufactures rubber tyres.)

dunny
A toilet, especially an outside toilet.

dunny budgie
An especially big blowfly.

dunny diver
A plumber.

durry
A cigarette.

dust-up
A punch-up or fight.

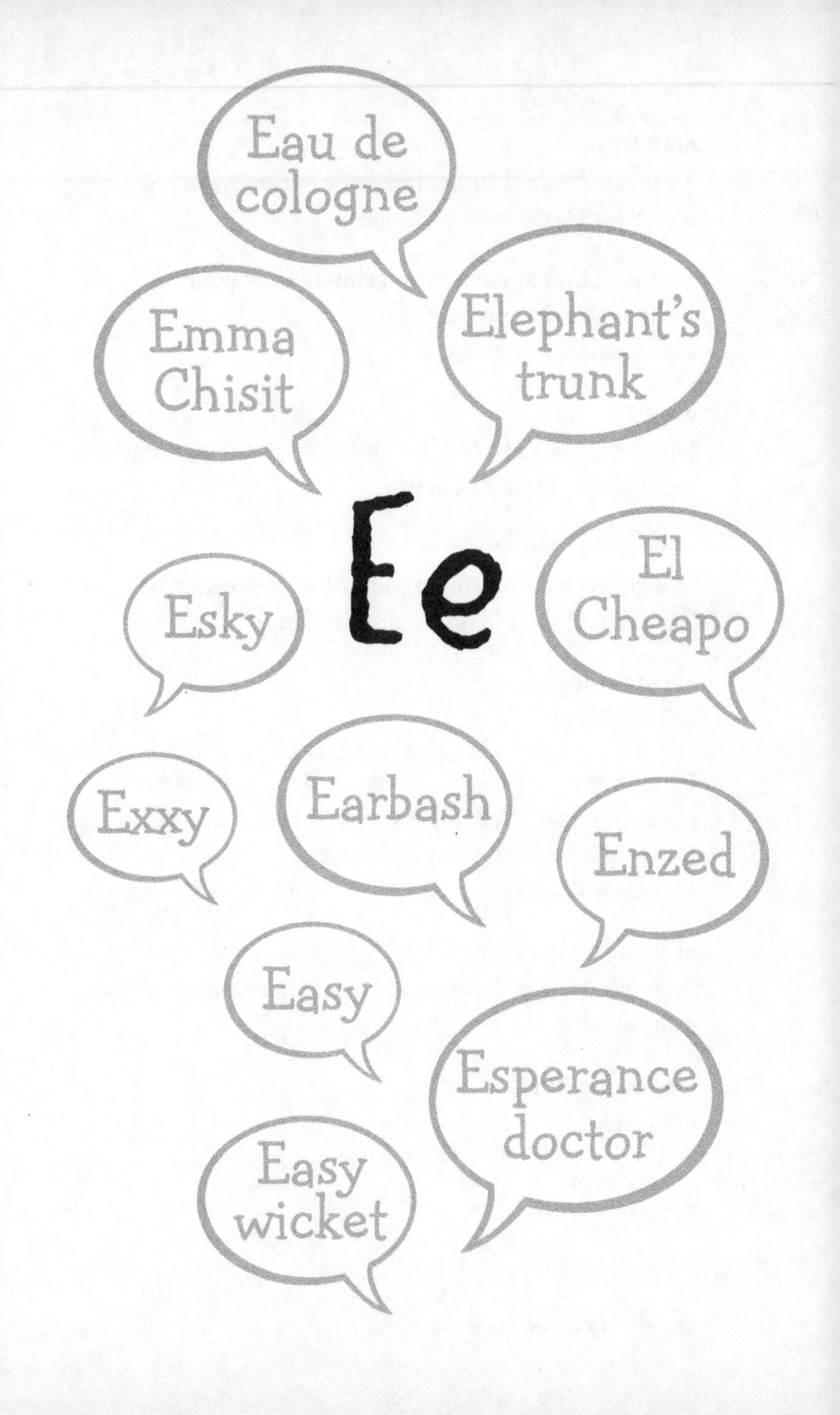
Eau de cologne
Emma Chisit
Elephant's trunk
Ee
Esky
El Cheapo
Exxy
Earbash
Enzed
Easy
Esperance doctor
Easy wicket

earbash
To talk incessantly, relentlessly or boringly. An *earbasher* is one who earbashes.

ears turn into arseholes and shit all over your shoulders, I hope your
joc. A curse.

easy
Unconcerned as to the outcome of a particular matter: e.g. 'I don't mind, I'm easy.'

easy wicket, on an
In a good or undemanding situation or position: e.g. 'With that job, he's on an easy wicket.'

eau de cologne
rs Telephone.

Edgar Britt
rs Shit. (Edgar Britt was a very successful Australian jockey in the 1930s, 40s and 50s.)
see also **brits**

el cheapo
Inexpensive: e.g. 'Let's go for an el cheapo meal at the pub tonight.'

elephant's trunk
rs Drunk.

Emerald City, the
Sydney. (From the play of that name by Australian playwright David Williamson. In the play, one of the characters describes Sydney as 'The Emerald city of Oz', because it doesn't hold the answers people hope to find there.)

Emma Chisit?
'How much is it?' (An example of Strine. From the 1960s when British author Monica Dickens was doing a book signing and mistook an Australian woman as giving the name 'Emma Chisit' to be inscribed in her copy of the book, when actually she was asking how much it cost.)

Enzed
New Zealand (from the acronym NZ). An *Enzedder* is someone from New Zealand.

esky
Any portable cooler for food and drinks (after the brand name).

Esperance doctor
A refreshing cool breeze blowing from the coastal town of Esperance to the hot inland town of Kalgoorlie in Western Australia.

excuse us!
int. Excuse me; pardon.

extra grouse
see **grouse**

E

exxy or **exy**
Expensive or dear.

eyes out, to go
To put in a lot of effort or the most effort possible.

Full of it
First crack
Feral
Fair crack of the whip
Full bore
Fella
FF
Flybog
Fit as a mallee bull
Fair dinkum
Flog
Fan-bloody-tastic!
Fosters flop
Fat as a match
Frog and toad
Footy

F

face fungus
Facial hair on a man: e.g. 'I hate kissing a man with face fungus, it's like kissing a toilet brush.'

face like a mallee root
A gnarled or ugly face. (The mallee eucalypt is an Australian tree with knotted and gnarled underground stems.)

fair dinkum
Genuine, honest and fair; truly.

fair enough
An expression of general approval or consent.

fair go
also fair crack of the whip; fair suck of the sav/sauce bottle
A fair or reasonable dealing. Often used as an appeal for someone to be more fair or reasonable: e.g. 'Fair go! There's no need to take that tone.'

fairy bread
A sweet treat often served at children's parties. Made from buttered white bread cut into triangles and sprinkled with coloured sprinkles or hundreds-and-thousands.

fairy floss
Spun sugar, usually served on a stick. Often sold at carnivals, fairs and fetes (known as candy floss in the UK and cotton candy in the US).

fan-bloody-tastic!
int. Fantastic! Excellent!

fang
1 To ask for a loan: e.g. 'The bugger fanged me for a grand!'
2 To drive a car fast: e.g. 'You'd better fang it if we're going to get there in time.'

fanny
A vagina.

fanta pants
A nickname for a red-headed person (after the orange-coloured soft drink).

fart in a bottle, couldn't
derog. Said of a useless or incompetent person.

fart in a bottle, like a
Very energetic, frenzied or spirited: e.g. 'That dog never stops running around the yard; he's like a fart in a bottle.'

fat as a butcher's dog
Very overweight.

fat as a match
Very thin.

Feds, the
abbrev. The Australian Federal Police.

feeding the chooks
(of a politician) To give irrelevant or unimportant information to the press, or to avoid directly answering a question that has been put. (Coined and practised by long-serving Queensland Premier Sir Joh Bjelke-Petersen.)

fella
abbrev. A man or bloke.

feral
1 Disgusting or dirty: e.g. 'The bathroom in that pub was so feral.'
2 Uncontrollable, disobedient or unruly: e.g. 'Their kids are totally feral.'
3 A hippy (insinuating that such a person is unkempt and unwashed).

ferret a run, give the
(of males) To have sexual intercourse. (Ferret is a nickname for penis.)

fibber
A liar.

fiddle-arse about
Waste time, dawdle or lag behind: e.g. 'Stop fiddle-arseing about, we're already running late!'

fight his/her way out of a paper bag, couldn't
also couldn't fight his/her way out of a wet paper bag
derog. Said of a stupid, incompetent or dim-witted person.

fight like a threshing machine
To fight energetically and forcefully.

firebug
A person who deliberately starts fires, especially bushfires.

firey
A firefighter.

first crack
First light; dawn.

First Fleet
hist. The ships that brought the first British settlers to Australia in 1788 (including many convicts as well as civilians).

First Fleeter
hist. Someone who arrived in Australia with the First Fleet. Nowadays taken to mean a person whose genealogy can be traced back to the First Fleet.

first in, best dressed
An expression indicating that the first person to arrive or participate has an advantage: e.g. 'Quick, head for the buffet table, it's first in best dressed.'

fit as a Mallee bull
also fit as a Mallee bull and twice as dangerous
Very fit or in robust health. (The Mallee refers to arid parts of southern Australia where mallee eucalypts are the predominant vegetation. Presumably the animals there are very hardy.)
see also **mallee root**

fiver
A $5 note: e.g. 'Can you lend me a fiver for the bus fare?'

fizgig or **fizzgig** or **phizgig**
A police informer.

fizzer
A failure or disappointment: e.g. 'The barbie was a fizzer – only three people turned up.'

fizz out on
Fail to follow through on a promise; to let down: e.g. 'I can't believe he fizzed out on me!'

flake
1 Any type of shark served in a fish and chip shop.
2 To pass out, often as a result of being intoxicated. (*also* flake out)

flaming
An intensifier, similar to bloody: e.g. 'What are you doing, ya flaming idiot!'

flange
A vagina.

flannie
A checked flannelette shirt, often worn by tradies and bogans.

flash
Stylish or showy: e.g. 'His new car's a bit flash.'

flash as a rat with a gold tooth
Dressed up or overdressed.

flat as a tack
Very flat.

flat-chat
Full pelt, very fast, or flat-out.

flat out like a lizard drinking
1 Very busy; working extremely hard.
2 Lying face down.

flick, to give something/someone the
To get rid of or reject: e.g. 'It just wasn't working out, so I gave him the flick.'

flicks, the
The cinema or the movies: e.g. 'Feel like going to the flicks later?'

flit, do a
To run away or to depart hastily and without warning.

F

flog
1 To steal: e.g. 'Someone flogged my car, so now I catch public transport to work.'
2 To sell or try to sell: e.g. 'He flogged it to the pawnshop.'

flog one's chops
To wear oneself out.

flossy up
To get dressed up or beautified.

fluff
1 A fart or the act of farting.
2 To make a mistake or error.
3 Something unimportant or frivolous. e.g. 'This book is just a bit of fluff, but it's entertaining.'

flyblown
Broke.

flybog
Jam.

fly country
Outback Australia.

flywire
also flyscreen
Mesh screens secured over windows and external doors to keep flies from entering.

footie or **footy**
1 The game of football, usually Australian Rules football.
2 A football.

footpath
A sidewalk or pedestrian walkway.

fortie or **forty**
A criminal or thief. (After *Ali Baba and the Forty Thieves.*)

fossick
To search for something in an unsystematic way. (Originally used to describe the search for surface gold in an area that had already been mined.)

Fosters flop
A man's inability to get an erection due to over-consumption of alcohol, usually beer. (Fosters Lager is a well-known Australian beer.)

fourby or **fourbie**
1 A four-wheel drive vehicle.
2 A four-by-two inch piece of timber.

four-legged lottery
Horseracing.

franger
A condom.

freckle
An anus.

Fred Nerk/s
also Fred Nurk/s
A hypothetical average man. (The equivalent of an American John Doe.)
see also **Joe Blow**

freebie
Something that is free or complimentary: e.g. 'We got heaps of cool freebies at the expo.'

freeze the balls off a brass monkey
see **cold enough to freeze the balls off a brass monkey**

Fremantle doctor
A refreshing cool breeze blowing from the coastal town of Fremantle to the city of Perth in Western Australia.

Freo
abbrev. Fremantle (a port city near Perth in Western Australia).

freshie
A freshwater crocodile.

frig
To masturbate.

frigging
An intensifier used to express displeasure: e.g. 'I can't get this frigging thing to work!'

frig-up

1 A mistake or muddle.

2 To make a mistake or make a mess of something: e.g. 'Well you frigged-up that job, they'll never hire us again.'

frog and toad

rs Road: e.g. 'Let's hit the frog and toad.'

from go to whoa

From start to finish: e.g. 'Their relationship went from go to whoa in about 5 minutes.'

fuckwit

derog. A stupid, nasty or irritating person.

fugly

Extremely ugly (a contraction of fucking ugly).

full as a goog

also full as a boot; full as a tick

1 Very drunk.

2 Full or unable to eat any more.

full bore

With the most effort, speed or enthusiasm possible.

full bottle, the

Said of someone who is very knowledgeable or skilled in a particular area. *Not the full bottle* refers to someone who lacks these qualities.

full of it, to be
To talk nonsense or be full of hot air: e.g. 'Stop boasting, you're so full of it.'

full-on
Extreme, serious, weighty or challenging: e.g. 'I can't believe he said that to you. That's really full-on.'

full quid, not the
Of lower-than-average intelligence, or not completely sane.

full-tilt
Flat-out; at maximum speed.

full up to dolly's wax
Completely full or satisfied after a meal.

funny as a fart in a phone box
Not at all funny.

furphy
hist. An untrue or false story; a rumour. (After the water carts made by J Furphy and Sons and used during World War I, around which soldiers gathered to exchange news and gossip.)

Galoot
Garbage guts
Game as Ned Kelly
Good
Galah
Goat-faced
Gg
Get a wriggle on!
Garbo
Gone to Gowings
Grouse
G'day
Go like the clappers
Grey nomads
Give it a burl
Get nicked!
Grog

G

G, the

abbrev. The MCG (Melbourne Cricket Ground), one of Australia's most famous and beloved sporting venues.

Gabba, the

The Brisbane Cricket Ground (an abbreviation of Woolloongabba, the suburb where the ground is located).

gagging for

In dire need of something: e.g. 'I'm gagging for a beer.'

galah

A silly, foolish or loud person. (After the native pink and grey cockatoo.)

galah session

Chat time on an outback radio service, when people in remote areas can talk to each other. (Galahs are noisy cockatoos that often gather in large flocks.)

galoot

A foolish or silly person.

game as a piss-ant

also game as a pebble

Very brave or courageous.

game as Ned Kelly

Very brave or cocky. (Ned Kelly was a much mythologised bushranger of the late 19th century.)

gammon
1 A deception or trick; a counterfeit.
2 To deceive, swindle or flatter.

garbage guts
A person who eats a lot or who will eat anything (including other peoples' scraps).

garbo
abbrev. A garbage collector.

gasper
A cigarette.

g'day
also gidday
abbrev. Good day. A casual way of saying 'Hello.'

gee-gees, the
Horseracing, specifically the horses: e.g. 'I think I'll put a bet on the gee-gees.'

geek
1 A nerdy or unfashionable person.
2 A look: e.g. 'Take a geek at that sheila.'

Germaine Greer
1 rs Beer.
2 rs Ear.
(Germaine Greer is an internationally renowned Australian writer and academic.)

get a wriggle on!
int. Hurry up! Get a move on!

get nicked!
int. Go away! Piss off!

get on one's tit/s
To annoy or irritate.

get stuck in/into
1 To begin a task with energy: e.g. 'Right, let's get stuck into the chores.'
2 To attack somebody, either verbally or physically.

getting any?
Have you been having any sex? (Normally asked of a man, by a man. Standard replies include: 'So busy I'm thinking of putting an extra man on!' and 'Climbing trees to get away from it!')

get with someone
To kiss or have sexual intercourse with someone: e.g. 'Did you get with him at the party?'

gibber
A stone or pebble. *Gibber country* refers to arid inland areas of Australia covered with stones.

gidday
see **g'day**

gig
1 To stare or observe.
2 A person who stares.

ginormous
Really gigantic or enormous.

give a rat's arse, I don't
also I don't give a rat's
I really don't care: e.g. 'I don't give a rat's arse what you think.'

give birth to a politician
To do a poo.

give it a bash
also give it a burl
To make an attempt at something, often with little confidence of success.

give it away
also give the game away
To give up or cease an activity, often through frustration.

give someone heaps
To give someone a hard time or insult them.

give the ferret a run
see **ferret a run, give the**

glad wrap
Any plastic cling wrap used in the kitchen. (After the GLAD brand of plastic wrap.)

glass door on a dunny
see **useful as a glass door on a dunny**

go and have a roll!
int. Get lost! Piss off!

goat-faced
Drunk.

gob
Mouth: e.g. 'Shut your gob!'

gobful
An earful: e.g. 'I gave him a real gobful when he finally showed up.'

go bush
To go into hiding, or take leave of one's community.

God
The nickname of celebrated former Aussie Rules football player Gary Ablett.

God-botherer
derog. A very religious person.

goer, a
A scheme or plan that is thought to be a good or promising one: e.g. 'I reckon your idea is a goer.'

go for your life
Go ahead; sure.

go like a cut cat
To do something very quickly or travel at speed: e.g. 'His new car goes like a cut cat.'

go like the clappers
To travel or work at great speed: e.g. 'We'll have to go like the clappers if we're going to get there on time.'

gollion
A gob of phlegm.

gone to Gowings
1 To have left hastily, suddenly or unexpectedly.
2 Crazy.
3 Penniless.
4 Unwell, especially after excessive drinking.
5 Drunk.
(From the 1940s advertising slogan for Gowings department stores.)

gong
An award or prize: e.g. 'I reckon he'll get a gong for that film.'

good guts
True or genuine information.

good iron!
also good ink
int. An exclamation of approval or pleasure.

good lurk, a
also not a bad lurk
A profitable or otherwise rewarding situation: e.g. 'You work a four-day week? That's a good lurk.'

good-oh or **goodo**
That's good; all right; fine.

good oil
The truth, good advice or useful information.

good onya!
also onya
int. Good on you! Well done!

good paddock, you've been in a
You've put on weight.

good sort
1 An attractive or sexually appealing person.
2 A good, kind or honest person.

good trot, a
A good or happy period or sequence of events.
see also **rough trot**

good value
(of a person) Entertaining, pleasant or likeable: e.g. 'Yeah, I really like Bazza, he's good value.'

go off
To be exciting, fun, in full swing or tremendously entertaining: e.g. 'The band was going off and everyone was dancing and jumping around.'

go off like a frog in a sock
Said of something that is a great success: e.g. 'The party went off like a frog in a sock.'

goog
An egg.

goom
Inexpensive alcohol, especially methylated spirits.

goon
see **cask wine**

goon bag
A bag which holds cask wine (i.e. the bag inside the box).

goondy or **goondie**
also gunyah
An Aboriginal hut or shelter; a humpy.

gorblimey!
also corblimey
int. An exclamation of astonishment or surprise.

Gordon Bennett!
int. An exclamation of frustration or astonishment. (Gordon Bennett was an Australian soldier who is particularly remembered for escaping from Singapore during WW II, leaving his men behind.)

got his/her licence out of a Weet-Bix packet
also got his/her licence out of a Corn Flakes packet
derog. Said of someone who seems unqualified to perform a task that normally requires a licence, such as driving a vehicle or working as a certified builder. (Weet-Bix is a popular brand of breakfast cereal.)
e.g. 'That accountant was so bad I reckon he got his licence out of a Weet-Bix packet.'

go two rounds with a revolving door, couldn't
Said of a stupid or useless person.

go walkabout
see **walkabout**

great Australian salute
also Australian salute; Aussie salute; one-handed salute
The action of waving one's hand in front of the face to get rid of flies.

green and gold
see **wear the green and gold**

greenie
An environmental activist, or any person who overtly expresses concern for the environment.

grey nomads
Retirees that travel around Australia by car. Usually found in the warmer states with a comfortably fitted-out caravan in tow.

grey nurse
An Australian $100 note (after the shark of that name and due to the colour of the note).

griff, the
The truth or honest advice.

grinning like a shot fox
Said of someone who is extremely pleased or satisfied, often smugly so.

grog
Alcohol. A *grog shop* is a liquor store.

grommet
A young or inexperienced surfer or snowboarder.

grouse
Excellent; very good. *Extra grouse* means really excellent.

g-string
An item of underwear comprising a small piece of fabric that covers the genitals, and a thin strip of cloth passed between the buttocks, leaving them bare. (The equivalent of a US thong.)

guernsey, get a
To be chosen for or invited to something, especially to play in an AFL team.

gullyraker
Cattle thief.

gumboots
also gummies; gumbies
Knee-high rubber wet-weather boots, equivalent to English wellingtons.

gum leaves growing out of one's ears, to have
To have lived in the bush a long time.

gum tree, up a
see **up a gum tree**

gun
A champion or best performer. Traditionally used to describe a champion sheep shearer, but nowadays used for just about anything: *gun pilot, gun lawyer, gun cyclist*.

gunna
A contraction of going to: e.g. 'I was gunna wash the car but then it started raining.'

gunyah
see **goondy**

gutful, to have had a
To have had enough or more than enough: e.g. 'I've had a gutful of your complaining.'

gutless wonder
A coward or wimp.

gyp
To con or deceive.

Hot to trot
Happy as Larry
Horse's doovers
Hum-dinger
Hh
Hooley dooley!
Home and hosed
Holus-bolus
Half your luck!
Heaps

had a few
Drunk: e.g. 'You better catch a taxi home because you've obviously had a few.'

halfback flanker
rs A wanker.

half-cut
also half-rinsed
Stupid or drunk.

half-pie
Worthless.

half your luck!
int. Congratulations! Well done! That's lucky for you. (An abbreviation of the phrase 'I wish I had half your luck'.)

handball
To avoid completing a task by passing or designating it to somebody else. (From the Aussie Rules term for passing the ball by hand from one player to another.)

happy as a bastard on Fathers' Day
Very unhappy.

happy as a dog with two tails
Very happy.

happy as Larry
Very happy.

happy little Vegemite
A happy or contented person, often a child. (From the 1950s advertising jingle for the popular Australian yeast spread Vegemite.) e.g. 'Your kids are happy little Vegemites today, aren't they?'
see also **axle grease**

hard case
A humorous or amusing person.

hard word on, to put the
see **put the bite on**

hard yakka
see **yakka**

hard yards, do the
also put in the hard yards
To work hard or put a lot of time and energy into something: e.g. 'You've done the hard yards, now it's time to sit back and enjoy.'

Harold Holt, do a
To disappear suddenly or under mysterious circumstances. (Harold Holt was an Australian prime minister who in 1967 disappeared while swimming in the ocean, and whose body was never found.)

hatful of worms
see **silly as a hatful of worms**

have a go, you mug!
also 'ave a go, ya mug!
int Hit the ball! (A taunt made by a cricket spectator to a batsman who isn't making many runs.)

have a slash
(of a man) To urinate.

have someone on
1 To kid or trick someone: e.g. 'No way! You're having me on!'
2 To fight someone.

have tickets on oneself
see **tickets on oneself**

Hawkesburies
rs The shivers. (Short for 'Hawkesbury rivers' – the Hawkesbury River is one of the major rivers in New South Wales.)

head like a dropped meat pie
also head like a slapped arse; head like a half-sucked mango; head like a drover's dog; head like a robber's dog; head like a busted watermelon; head like a chewed Mintie; head like a bucket of smashed crabs
Said of a person who is particularly unattractive.

heaps
A lot: e.g. 'There were heaps of people there.'

heaps, give someone
see **give someone heaps**

heart as big as Phar Lap
Said of a very generous or loving person. (Phar Lap was a successful and much heroised Australian racehorse, whose heart was almost twice as big as that of a normal racehorse.)

heart-starter
An alcoholic beverage, usually consumed early in the day.

hens' night
The female equivalent of a bucks' night; i.e. an evening of entertainment and drinking attended by a bride and her female friends before her wedding day.

hide the sausage, to play
(of a man) To have sexual intercourse.

hills hoist
Any rotary clothesline. (After the brand name of the first such clothesline, invented in Australia by Lance Hill in the 1940s.)

hit and giggle
Any sport played socially or just for enjoyment, especially a game that requires a bat or racket: e.g. 'I'm off to the tennis club for a bit of hit and giggle with the girls.'

hit for six
see **knocked for six**

hive off
To depart.

Hobartian
A person from Hobart, the state capital of Tasmania.

hock
To pawn: e.g. 'I had to hock my guitar to get some cash.'

hoe into
1 To undertake in an enthusiastic or energetic manner: e.g. 'Look at him hoe into that burger!'
2 To attack or abuse verbally.

hoick
To spit.

hold your horses!
int. Wait a minute! Hang on!

hole, a
A rundown or unappealing place or venue. 'Did you see the peeling paint in their living room? What a hole!'

hols
also hollies
Holidays; holiday period: e.g. 'Are you going away for the hols?'

holus-bolus
All at the same time; everything at once.

home and hosed
hist. Finished or completed successfully. (Originally used to describe a horse that won a race by such a long way that it was already 'home and hosed down' by the time the other horses finished.)

home on the pig's back
Easily accomplished.

honk
To smell bad.

Honkers
abbrev. Hong Kong.

hook one's bait
To leave or depart.

hooley dooley!
int. A bright exclamation of surprise.

hoon
A hooligan, lout or show-off; especially one who drives at excessive speed and/or dangerously.

hooroo! or **ooroo!**
int. Goodbye!

hop
A police officer.

hope your balls turn into bicycle wheels and back pedal up your arse
see **balls turn into bicycle wheels**

hope all your chooks turn into emus and kick your house/dunny down
see **chooks turn into emus**

hope your ears turn into arseholes and shit all over your shoulders
see **ears turn into arseholes**

horse's doovers
A deliberate mispronunciation of 'hors d'oeuvres.'

hostie
An air hostess or flight attendant.

hot, not so
see **not so hot**

hot as Hay, hell and Booligal
Extremely hot. (After the poem by beloved Australian bush poet 'Banjo' Paterson, titled *Hay and Hell and Booligal.* Hay and Booligal are small rural towns in far western New South Wales.)

hottie
1 A hot-water bottle.
2 A sexually attractive person.

hot to trot
Eager to begin.

howzat!
int. Literally 'How is that?' In cricket, an enthusiastic appeal to the umpire that a batsman is out.

humdinger
A wonderful or terrific person or thing.

hump
1 To carry. (Historically used in the phrase *to hump a bluey* – a bluey being the bundle carried by a tramp or swagman.)
2 To have sexual intercourse.

humpy
A small shelter or shack, often temporary. Often used to describe the bush dwellings used by Aborigines.

hungry
Selfish or nasty.

hurl
To vomit.

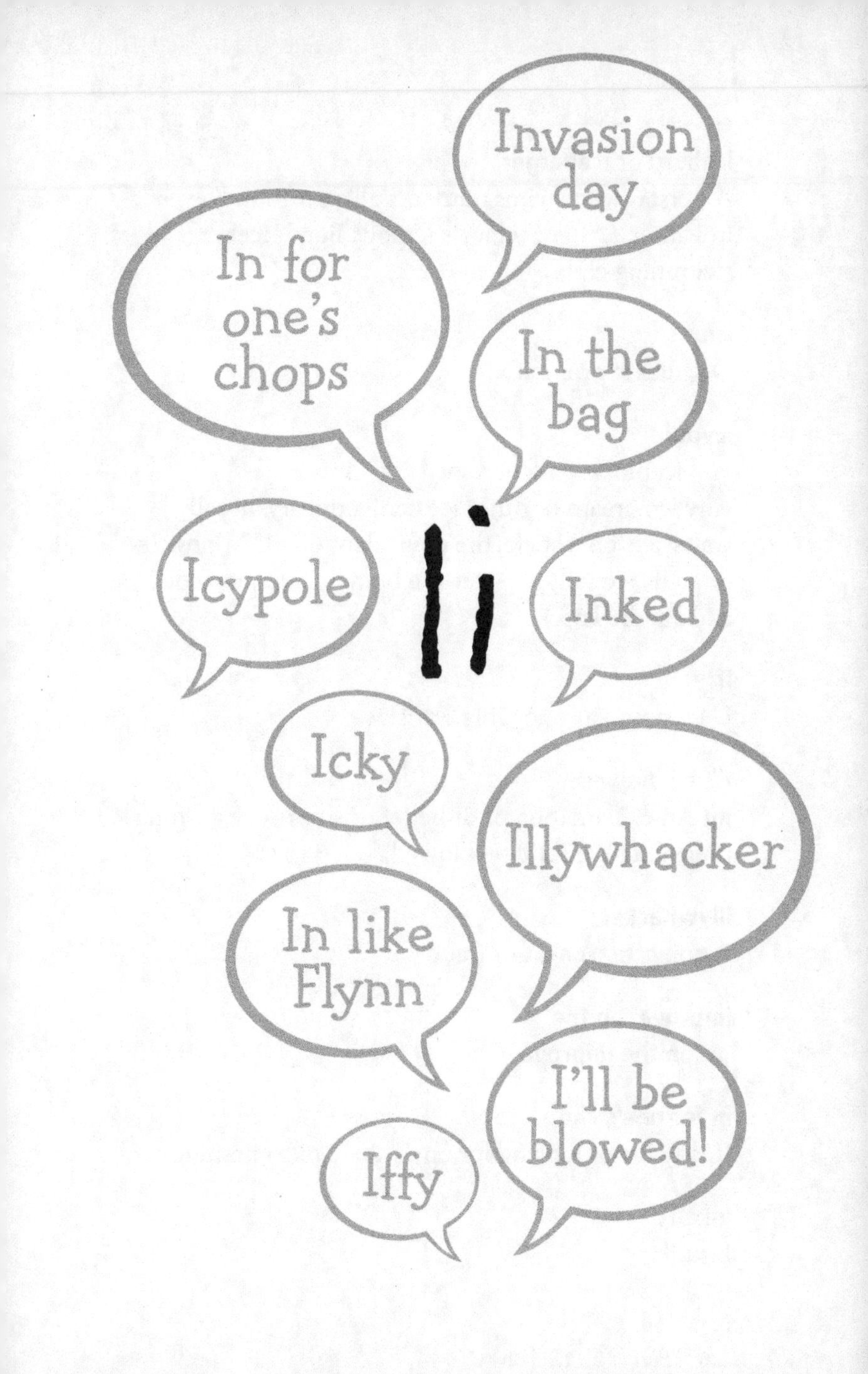
Invasion day
In for one's chops
In the bag
Icypole
Ii
Inked
Icky
Illywhacker
In like Flynn
I'll be blowed!
Iffy

I

iceberg or **iceberger**
A person who swims outdoors all-year round, even in winter. (After Sydney's famous Bondi Icebergs swimming club.)

icky
Disgusting or gross.

icypole
also iceblock; paddle pop
Any ice-cream or other ice confectionary, usually water ice, on a stick (the equivalent of a US popsicle or a UK ice lolly). (After the brand names, Icy Pole and Paddle Pop.)

iffy
Uncertain, questionable or risky.

I'll be blowed!
int An exclamation of disbelief or surprise: e.g. 'You're pregnant? We'll I'll be blowed!'

illywhacker
A con artist, cheat or fraud.

improve, on the
see **on the improve**

in for one's chop
Ready for or looking for one's share of something.

inked
Drunk.

in like Flynn
Enthusiastic, eager or quick to act, often in relation to a sex; likely to succeed or achieve something. (After Australian actor Errol Flynn, who was a notorious womaniser.)

innings
A period of time or a turn at something (from the cricketing term): e.g. 'My grandfather died at 91 years of age, so he had a pretty good innings.'

in the bag
A certain or guaranteed outcome: e.g. 'This game's in the bag, they'll never beat us now.'

in the chair, to be
To be the one whose turn it is to pay for a round of drinks.

Invasion Day
A sardonic term for Australia Day (the day set aside to celebrate the first European [British] settlement of Australia).

Jiminy crickets
Jackaroo
Jaffle
Jj
Jumbuck
Jumpy as a wallaby
Jim-jams
Jeez!
Just quietly

J

jack

1 A policeman. (*also* john; john hop)
2A kookaburra (an Australian species of kingfisher). (An abbreviation of 'laughing jackass'); (*also* jacko)
3 Nothing: e.g. 'He knows jack shit about women.' (*also* jack shit)
4 *Jack of* means sick of or had enough of: e.g. 'I'm jack of doing these chores.'

jack and jill

rs The bill: e.g. 'Shall I ask the waiter for the jack and jill?'

jackaroo or **jackeroo**

A young man working on a sheep or cattle station in order to gain training and experience.
cf. jillaroo.

Jackie Howe

A name for the popular navy-blue singlets worn by Australian labourers and farm workers. (After Jackie Howe, who broke all shearing records in the 1890s, allegedly while wearing such a singlet.)

jack of

see **jack**

jackshay or **jackshea**

see **billy**

jaffle
Any toasted-sandwich maker or toasted sandwich, especially one with sealed edges. (After the jaffle irons historically used to toast sandwiches over the camp fire.)

jagging, go
To make a social visit or phone call, usually with the intention of spreading or gathering gossip.

jamboree
A gathering or celebration, often a noisy one.

jar
A glass of beer.

jarmies
see **jim-jams**

JC
acr. Jesus Christ.

jeez!
also jees; geez
int. An exclamation of frustration, annoyance or surprise (from 'Jesus'): e.g. 'Jeez, did you see how fast that hoon was going?'

jillaroo or **jilleroo**
A young woman working on a sheep or cattle station in order to gain training and experience.
cf. jackaroo.

J

jiminy crickets
also jiminies
rs Tickets.

jim-jams
also jarmies
Pyjamas.

Jimmy Brit
rs Shit.
see also **brits**

Joe Blake
rs A snake.

Joe Blakes, the
rs The shakes, especially delirium tremens.

Joe Blow
also Joe Bloggs
A hypothetical average man. (The equivalent of an American John Doe.)
see also **Fred Nerk**

joes, the
The blues; feelings of sadness or dejection.

joey
An infant marsupial (e.g. kangaroo, possum, wombat or koala): e.g. 'That roo has a joey in her pouch.'

John Dory
rs Story: e.g. 'What's the John Dory?'

Johnny Bliss
rs Piss.

journo
abbrev. Journalist.

jumbuck
A sheep. (This word is perhaps best known nowadays from Australia's informal national anthem, 'Waltzing Matilda', for example in the following lines: 'And he sang as he stowed that jumbuck in his tucker bag/ You'll come a-waltzing Matilda with me.')

jumper
The equivalent of a US sweater or pullover.

jumpy as a wallaby
Said of a person who is very anxious or edgy.

just quietly
Just between you and me; in confidence: e.g. 'Just quietly, I reckon their marriage is on the rocks.'

Kick the tin
Kanga bangers
Knock off
Knock rotten
King-hit
Kk
Kick and giggle
Keen as mustard
Keep nit
Knickers
Knocked for six
Kick on
Keep out of the rain

K

k
abbrev. Kilometre: e.g. 'It's just a few k's down the road, you can't miss it.'

kanakas
Testicles.

kanga
abbrev. Kangaroo.

kanga bangers
Sausages made with kangaroo meat.

kangaroos loose in the top paddock, a few
Said of a stupid or dim-witted person.

kark it
see **cark it**

keen as mustard
Extremely keen or eager.

keep down
To hold onto or retain, especially employment: e.g. 'Her husband just can't keep down a job.'

keep nit
Keep watch; be on lookout.

keep one's end up
To hold up one's end of a bargain, or play one's part.

keep out of the rain
Stay out of trouble.

kelly
1 A crow.
2 An axe.

kelpie
A hardy shorthaired breed of Australian sheepdog, originally developed from Scottish collie dogs.

kick
A wallet: e.g. 'Hit your kick' (open your wallet).

kick and giggle
derog. Aussie Rules football.

kick in
Contribute or give: e.g. 'Let's all kick in and get them a really nice wedding gift.'

kick off
To die.

kick on
To continue celebrating at a party or gathering, normally late into the evening. e.g. 'The shivoo we went to last night was great. We kicked on 'til dawn.'

kick the arse off an emu, could
Said of someone who's on form and ready for any challenge.

kick the tin
To make a donation.

kiddies
also kiddiewinks; kiddliewinks
Children.

kid-stakes
A small or unimportant matter.

killer, the
The final straw or knock-out blow.

king dick
The boss or person in charge.

king-hit
To strike or punch unexpectedly and forcefully, often from behind: e.g. 'I was king-hit outside the nightclub.'

kip
A brief sleep or snooze.

kiss and cuddle
also catch and kiss
derog. Soccer.

Kiwi
1 A person from New Zealand.
2 Relating to New Zealand: e.g. 'The kiwi accent sure is funny.'
(After the flightless bird that is native to New Zealand.)

knackered
Very tired or worn out.

knickers
Women's underpants.

knock
1 To have sexual intercourse.
2 To criticise: e.g. 'Don't knock it until you've tried it.'

knockabout
1 A person who's had a hard life and is a bit rough around the edges.
2 A tramp or drifter; a station handyman or itinerant worker.

knock back
1 To decline or reject. A *knock-back* is a rebuff.
2 To imbibe a drink: e.g. 'We knocked back a few tinnies after work.'

knocked for six
also hit for six
Surprised or astonished (from cricketing, where a ball hit over the boundary scores six points): e.g. 'You could've knocked me for six when she told me about her new job.'

knockers
Breasts.

knock it off!
int. Stop it! That's enough!

K

knock off

1 To finish or stop: e.g. 'Meet me after work, I knock off at six.'

2 To steal: e.g. 'Someone knocked off my bike.'

3 A *knockoff* is a replica or counterfeit: e.g. 'The watch was only $10, because it's a knockoff.'

knock rotten

To defeat by a wide margin.

knock-shop

A brothel.

knock something on the head, to

To put a stop to something, especially at an early stage or before it has gone too far: e.g. 'I could see his plan wasn't going to work, so I knocked the idea on the head.'

know his arse from his elbow, doesn't

Said of a stupid or dim-witted person.

knuckle, go the

To have a fight, especially using the fists.

Little tacker
Lob in
Lunatic soup
Lousy as a bandicoot
Laughing jackass
Larrikin
Ll
London to a brick
Lamb-brained
Lucky Country
Loo
Liquid laugh
Lair up
Land lice
Lecky blanket
Lubricate the larynx
Let her rip
Lung buste

L

lackie band
also lacky band; lacker band
An elastic/rubber band.

Lady Muck
A woman who is arrogant and self-important, or puts on airs: e.g. 'Look at Lady Muck over there, relaxing while everyone else works.'

lair
A flashy, ostentatious, offensive young man. *To lairise* is to behave in a flashy, ostentatious, offensive way.

lair up
To dress up for an occasion; to dress flashily: e.g. 'We got all laired up to go dancing.'

lamb-brained
Foolish or stupid.

lamington drive
Any fundraising cake sale. (From the Australian lamington cake: a cube of sponge cake dipped in chocolate icing and then coated with desiccated coconut.)

land lice
derog. Sheep.

larrikin
An unruly, mischievous or undisciplined person, usually male. Often *lovable larrikin*.

Larry Dooley, give someone the
To chastise someone, either physically or verbally. (Larry Dooley was a successful Australian boxer.)

Larry Dooley, give it the
To give something extra effort.

lash at, have a
To have a go at; to attempt or participate in something.

laughing gear
Mouth: e.g. 'Wrap your laughing gear around this' (i.e. 'Eat this').

laughing jackass
A kookaburra (an Australian bird with a loud, distinctive call or 'laugh').

lay-by
To put a small deposit on an item to reserve it, then pay it off with periodic payments: e.g. 'The shoes were a bit pricey, so I put them on lay-by.'

leadfoot
A person who habitually drives at excessive speed.

leave for dead, to
To leave behind, especially in a race: e.g. 'I left them for dead in the hurdles.'

lecky blanket
An electric blanket for warming one's bed.

legless
Extremely drunk, to the point of no longer being able to stand up.

legs, to have
To have potential or credibility (especially of a scheme or plan).

lemon
A dud; something that is broken or faulty from the outset: e.g. 'The car turned out to be a lemon.'

lemon squash
1 A lemon-flavoured soft drink.
2 rs Wash.

lemony
Angry or annoyed.

let her rip
also let it rip
Give it a go; fire it up; let's get started.

lie straight in bed, couldn't
derog. Said of a dishonest person or liar.

lift one's game
also pull one's socks up
To improve one's performance or behaviour: e.g. 'You'd better lift your game son, or you'll be kicked off the team.'

li-lo
Any inflatable air mattress (after the LI-LO brand name).

lingo
Language or jargon.

Lionel Rose
rs Nose. (Lionel Rose was a famous Indigenous Australian boxer of the 1960s.)

liquid amber
Beer.

liquid laugh
Vomit.

liquid lunch
A lunch that only includes alcohol, usually beer.

little Aussie battler
see **battler.**

little boys
Cocktail frankfurts.

little tacker
A child: e.g. 'I think I'll take the little tacker fishing with me this weekend.'

littlies
Children: e.g. 'Give us a hand bathing the littlies.'

Lizzie Windsor
Queen Elizabeth II.

loaded
1 Wealthy.
2 Drunk.

lob in
To arrive unexpectedly or unannounced.

lobster
A $20 note (due to the orange colour of the note).

lolly
A sweet; any kind of confectionery: e.g. 'There were heaps of lollies at the party: toffees, chocolates, jubes and liquorice.'

lolly, to do one's
also to go off one's lolly
To become enraged.

lolly bag
A bag of lollies (sweets) given to children at the end of a party to take home with them.
see also **budgie smugglers**

lolly water
Soft drink, or any very sweet drink.

London to a brick on
also London to a brick; bet London to a brick
Said of something that is highly likely or a certainty (originally a horseracing term): e.g. 'London to a brick that drongo will be fired by the end of the week.'

lonely as a bandicoot on a burnt ridge
see **bandicoot on a burnt ridge**

lonely as a country dunny
also all alone like a country dunny
Very lonely; alone.

loo
A toilet.

loop the loop
rs Soup.

lose one's meal
To vomit.

lose the plot
To become confused or irrational.

lousy as a bandicoot
Said of someone who is really mean with money.

lower than a snake's belly
Said of a person who is really contemptible or corrupt.

lubricate the larynx
To imbibe an alcoholic beverage, usually a beer.

L

Lucky Country, the
Australia. (From the title of a book by the late Australian author Donald Horne. He used the term ironically, but it has been adopted as a positive description.)

lug someone's ear
To borrow money from someone.

lumbered with, to be
To be burdened or left with, especially with something unpleasant: e.g. 'We were lumbered with babysitting the grandkids again.'

lunatic soup
Alcohol.

lung buster
A cigarette.

lurk
see **good lurk**

Mateship
Moccas
Mopoke
Myster
meat
Muster
Maggot pack
Mm
Molly-dooker
Mad as a cut snake
Mug
Mongrel
More front than Myers
Moo juice
Mopey as a wet hen
Mystery bag
Mo

M

Macca
A nickname for any man whose surname begins with 'Mc' or 'Mac'.

mad as a cut snake
also mad as a gum tree full of galahs; mad as a maggot; mad as a meat axe
Crazy, mad, angry or stupid.

mad as a goanna
Daft or stupid.

mad Mick
rs Pick.

maggoted
Extremely drunk.

maggot pack
A meat pie.

maggoty
Irritable or bad-tempered.

magpie
A person from South Australia (after the black and white bird of that name).

magsman
An old-fashioned term for a chatty or overly talkative person.

make a box of
To make a mess of or confuse.

Mallee bull
see **fit as a Mallee bull**

Mallee root
rs A prostitute.

malt sandwich
A beer imbibed in place of a meal.

manchester
Household linen such as bed sheets, bath towels, tea towels etc. (After the city of Manchester in England, which was historically the hub of the British cotton industry.)

man in white
An umpire, especially in a game of cricket.

man with no hands, like a
Like a miserly or stingy person: e.g. 'He throws his money around like a man with no hands!'

Maoriland
New Zealand.

map of Tasmania
also map of Tassie; map of Tazzie
Female pubic hair, deemed to resemble the roughly triangular shape of Australia's southern island state.

mark
A type of catch in Australian Rules football. (Marking is a distinctive and often spectacular part of the game,

as players leap high into the air, sometimes springing off the back or shoulders of a teammate or opponent, to take the mark).

mate

Friend, buddy, pal, partner. A famous Australian form of address used mainly by men when talking to anybody from close friends to complete strangers. 'G'day mate, could I get a couple of coldies and a packet of chips thanks?'

mateship

An alleged trait of the Aussie character, suggesting loyalty, friendship and a fair-go attitude.

mates' rates

A discounted or cheaper rate for something, received from or given to a friend or acquaintance.

Matilda

hist. A roll of personal belongings carried by a swagman (made famous by Banjo Paterson's popular folk song 'Waltzing Matilda').

may all your chooks turn into emus and kick your dunny down

also may your balls turn into bicycle wheels and back-pedal up your arse; may your ears turn into arseholes and shit all over your shoulders

joc. A curse.

mazuma

Money.

meat pies short of a grand final, a couple of
Said of a stupid or dim-witted person. (Meat pies are the traditional staple of spectators at Australian Rules football games, and the biggest game of the year is the grand final.)

Melba
see **Nellie Melba.**

Melburnian or **Melbournian**
A person from Melbourne, the state capital of Victoria.

Mexican
For someone living in New South Wales, a Mexican is any person living 'south of the border' in Victoria. For those in Queensland, the term also includes anyone in New South Wales.

Mickey Mouse
rs Grouse.

mince pies
rs Eyes.

min min
Mysterious lights seen in eastern Australia, thought to be some kind of unexplained natural phenomenon.

Mighty Murray, the
The Murray River. (The Murray is Australia's second-longest river, and marks the border between the states of Victoria and New South Wales.)

M

milk bar
A small local shop selling milk, bread, sweets, snacks and other groceries.

Mintie, without a
Broke, penniless. (Minties are an Australian brand of mint-flavoured lollies.)

miserable as a bandicoot
Really miserable.

mite
A young child.

mix it
To fight.

mo
1 **abbrev.** Moment: e.g. 'Hold on, I'll be with you in a mo.'
2 **abbrev.** Moustache.

mob
Any group of people or animals, but especially kangaroos.

moccas
abbrev. Moccasins; especially those made from sheepskin with the fleece retained on the inside.

mockered up
Dressed up: e.g. 'She was all mockered up for her big date.'

molies
abbrev. Moleskin trousers (comfortable, heavy-duty cotton pants that were traditionally stockman's apparel, but are now worn by many urban-dwellers).

mollydooker or **mollyduker**
also mollydook
A left-handed person.

molly the monk
rs Drunk.

money-spinner
An enterprise that makes, or is intended to make, a lot of money: e.g. 'Fixing up these old cars has been a real money-spinner.'

mongrel
1 An unpleasant, unkempt or contemptible person: e.g. 'Get out of here, you mongrel!'
2 Courage or guts: e.g. 'Show a bit of mongrel!'

monkey bars
A formation of bars for children to climb and play on, usually found in outdoor playgrounds: e.g. 'She fell off the monkey bars at school and broke her wrist.'

monte
also monty
An inevitability or certainty.

month of Sundays, dull as a
also boring as a month of Sundays
Very dull or boring.

moo juice
Milk.

moosh
Mouth.

mopey as a wet hen
Miserable or down in the dumps.

mopoke
A stupid, mopey, dull or slow person. (After an owl found in Australia and New Zealand.)

more arse than class
Said of something that has come about more through luck or chance than skill or preparation: e.g. 'Their win in the competition was more arse than class.'

more front than Myers, have
also have more front than a row of shops
To have a lot of audacity, nerve or attitude (Myer is an Australian chain of large department stores): e.g. 'I can't believe how rude that girl is, she's got more front than Myers!'

more hair on your chest!
int. An expression of encouragement, from man to man.

more shit than a Werribee duck, in
To be in strife or in a lot of trouble. (The suburb of Werribee in Victoria is home to a large sewage-treatment plant.)

Morts Dock
rs A cock (penis).

mossie or **mozzie**
A mosquito.

mother-in-law
A rag: e.g. 'Grab a couple of mother-in-laws and start cleaning those windows.'

motsa or **motser** or **motza**
A lot of money, especially money won through gambling.

mott
To watch or stare.

mouth like a camel-driver's crutch, to have a
also to have a mouth like the bottom of a cocky's cage
To have a very dry mouth, especially the morning after a big drinking session.

Mrs Kafoops or **Mrs Kerfoops**
Used to refer to a woman whose name you don't know: e.g. 'That Mrs Kafoops down the street is always screaming at her husband.'

M

muck up
1 To misbehave or play up
2 To ruin or spoil.

muck-up day
The last day of high school for final-year students during which they run riot and play pranks on the rest of the school.

muddie or **muddy**
A Queensland mud crab, also known as a mangrove crab, which is considered a culinary delicacy.

mud map
A rough or sketchy map. (Originally a map drawn on the ground with a stick.)

mug
A foolish or gullible person. A *mug punter* is an inexperienced or unsuccessful gambler.

mulga, the
Any remote region. By extension, *mulga madness* is mental derangement owing to extreme isolation. (Mulga is a common name for the scrubby vegetation typical of dry inland areas of Australia.)

mullygrubber
In cricket, a ball that when bowled hits the ground and rolls or skids along, rather than bouncing.

mum
also mummy
Mother: e.g. 'What's your mum making for dinner?'

murder a beer, I could
I really feel like a beer.

muso
abbrev. Musician.

muster
To round up livestock, especially cattle or sheep.

mystery bag
rs Snag (sausage). (From the suspected dubious quality and type of meat used.)

mystery meat
The meat used to make a meat pie or sausage. (From the suspected dubious quality and type of meat used.)

myxo
abbrev. Myxomatosis. (A disease introduced to control the plague-like numbers of environmentally-damaging rabbits in Australia.)

No worries
Not the full two-bob
Nick off!
Not cricket
Nn
No flies on him!
No probs
No good to gundy
Nutty as a fruitcake
Nanna
Nosh up

N

nads
abbrev. Gonads (testicles).

nags
also the nags
Horses, especially racehorses, or horseracing generally.

nanna
also nan
Grandmother.

nappie or **nappy**
The equivalent of a US diaper.

narked or **narky**
Irritable or in a bad mood.

nasty piece of work
A malicious, mean or generally horrid person.

nature strip
In suburban areas, a strip of grass planted between a footpath and a road: e.g. 'I can't believe the neighbours dumped their old TV out on the nature strip instead of taking it to the tip!'

ned
rs Head: e.g. 'You need to think this through. Come on, use your ned.'

neddies, the
Horses, especially racehorses or horseracing generally: e.g. 'I think I'll have a flutter on the neddies.'

neenish tart
also nienish tart; nenish tart
A small sweet tart iced with two colours, usually chocolate and white or chocolate and pink.

nellie or **nelly**
Wine, especially cheap or poor quality wine.

Nellie Blighs
rs Flies or blowflies.

Nellie Melba, do a
also do a Melba
A repeated undertaking to leave, never fulfilled. (After the succession of 'farewell' concerts given by legendary Australian opera singer Nellie Melba in the 1930s.)

nervous as a mother roo in a room full of pickpockets
Very nervous. (Female kangaroos carry their young in a pocket-like pouch.)

Never Never, the
Australia's remote inland areas.

Neville, a
also a Nigel
An unfashionable or geeky person.

new chum
1 A recently arrived immigrant, especially one from the UK.
2 A beginner or inexperienced person.

nice cup of tea, a Bex and a good lie down
To need a nice cup of tea, a Bex and a good lie down is to be fed up, tired or discontented. (Bex was a brand of analgesic purportedly popular with housewives in the 1950s and 60s.)

New South Welshman/Welshwoman
A man/woman from New South Wales.

nick, do a
To escape or flee.

nick off
1 To leave or depart.
2 int. Get lost!

nightie
A nightdress.

nipper
A junior lifesaver.

Noah's Ark
also Noah
rs A shark.

no Arthur Murrays
rs No worries. (Arthur Murray started a popular chain of dance studios in the 1920s.)

no drama/s
No worries; that's no big deal.

no flies on him/her
Said of a person considered to be intelligent or shrewd.

no good to gundy
No good to anybody.

no great shakes
Nothing wonderful; not very impressive or good.

no-hoper
A person considered to be a failure or a loser.

nong or **ning-nong**
A silly, simple or stupid person (often used in a light-hearted manner).

no picnic
Used to describe something difficult or unpleasant: e.g. 'Working as a brickie is no picnic.'

no probs
abbrev. No problem: e.g. 'I can fix that for you, no probs.'

norks
also norgs; norgies
Breasts.

Norm, a
An average Aussie bloke, especially one who is lazy and obese. (From the cartoon character of that name who featured in the public 'Life. Be in it.' get-fit campaign that began in the 1970s.)

N

north island, the
For Tasmanians, the rest of Australia.

North Shore tank
derog. A four-wheel drive (off-road) vehicle owned by a city dweller and mostly (or only) driven in the suburbs. (The North Shore is a wealthy area of Sydney.)
cf. Toorak tractor

nosh-up
A large or satisfying meal.

not a bad sort
A decent, attractive or likeable person.

not a skerrick
see **skerrick**

not bad
also not too bad
Good.

not cricket
also just not cricket
Not proper, just or right.

not enough sense to come in out of the rain
Said of a very stupid or unintelligent person.

not half bad
Very good or exceptional.

not happy, Jan!
int. An expression of irritation or annoyance (from a 2001 television advertisement for the Yellow Pages).

not much chop
Not very good; disappointing.

not on your Nelly!
also not on your Nellie
int. No way! Not on your life!

not the full two-bob
Said of someone who is unintelligent or not completely sane.

not so hot
Not very well or good, especially not feeling very well.

not worth a cracker
see **cracker**

no worries
Don't worry; you're welcome; that's not a problem; don't worry about it; okay; yes.

no wucking furries
also no wucking ferries; no wuckers; no wukkas
No worries. (A deliberate spoonerism of 'no fucking worries'.)

NSW
acr. New South Wales.

N

NT
acr. Northern Territory.

nuddy, in the
In the nude; naked.

nuggety
Short, stubby or stocky: e.g. 'He's a nuggety bloke, but he can run like the wind.'

nutty as a fruitcake
Mad or crazy.

NZ
acr. New Zealand.

On a good wicket
Ocker
Oi!
Oo
On one's Pat
Onka-paringas
Oz
Out bush
Open-air wrestling
Out for a duck

O

ocker
A person considered to typify the uncouth Australian character, and who is likely to be ignorant or uncultivated.

off like a bride's nightie
also off like a bucket of prawns in the sun
Said of a person who departs hurriedly or quickly: e.g. 'As soon as the beer ran out, he was off like a bride's nightie.'

off one's brain
also off one's head
Raving or upset, often with anger.

off one's face
To be intoxicated to the point of losing control.

offsider
also sidekick
Partner, assistant or hanger-on: e.g. 'That's the mechanic's offsider.'

oi!
int. A call to get someone's attention: e.g. 'Oi! We're over here!'

oil
Information, news, gossip or advice.
see also good oil

oily rag, on the smell of an
see **smell of an oily rag**

Old Country, the
also the Old Dart
For many Australians it refers to Britain, especially England. Nowadays often used sardonically.

oldies
also olds
Old people, often one's parents: e.g. 'Are you inviting the oldies to the barbie?'

on a good wicket
To be in a situation that is, or is likely to be, useful or profitable.

on a ham and cheese
To be on a roll, or onto something good.

on at, to be
also to go on at
To berate, reprimand or nag: e.g. 'She's always on at me about mowing the lawn.'

one-eyed trouser snake
joc. A penis. (A term used by Australian entertainer Barry Humphries, best known for his parodic character Dame Edna Everage.)

one-handed saluted
see **great Australian salute**

one-legged man in an arse-kicking competition, busy as a
see **busy as a blue-arsed fly**

one-legged man in an arse-kicking competition, useful as a
see **useful as a one-legged man in an arse-kicking competition**

one out of the bag
also one out of the box
An exceptional person or thing.

on for young and old
Used to describe a state of chaos, confusion or a fracas: e.g. 'Someone taunted the team captain and then it was on for young and old.'

onkaparingas
also onkas
rs Fingers. (Onkaparinga is a longstanding Australian brand of blanket, as well as the name of a city in South Australia.)

onkus
Not right, broken or wrong.

on one's ace
On one's own.

on one's ear
Drunk.

on one's Pat
rs Alone. (Short for 'on one's Pat Malone'.)

on the blink
Playing up or not working properly: e.g. 'The bloody telly's on the blink again.'

on the improve
Improving, recovering or looking up.

on the Murray
rs On credit. (Short for 'on the Murray cod', which is rhyming slang for 'on the nod'.)

on the nose
also on the bugle
Smelly. By extension, unpopular, contemptible, unpleasant or unwanted.

on the piss
also on the turps
On a drinking spree. *To get on the piss/turps* is to go on a drinking spree.

on ya!
see **good on ya!**

ooroo!
see **hooroo!**

open-air wrestling
derog. Rugby (normally used by fans of Australian Rules football).

open slather
A situation or opportunity that is open to anybody and everybody, and likely to have few rules or restrictions; a free-for-all.

op shop
abbrev. An opportunity shop, i.e. a second-hand or charity shop.

optic
rs Perv (look). (Short for 'optic nerve'.)

organise a chook raffle in a country pub, couldn't
also couldn't organise a fart in a curry house/chilli-eating competition; couldn't organise a pissup in a brewery
Said of a disorganised, stupid or useless person.

OS
abbrev. Overseas: e.g. 'I went travelling OS for a year after high school.'

Oscar Asche
rs Cash. (Oscar Asche was an Australian stage actor, producer and writer in the early 1900s.)

outback, the
The vast remote inland areas of Australia.

out bush
Any remote or isolated area.

out for a duck
Unsuccessful or ineffective, especially on a first attempt at something. (From the cricketing term, which applies when a batsman is dismissed without making a single run.)

outlaws
In-laws.

out of it
Distracted, inebriated, vague or not paying attention.

overhung
Hung-over.

overland
To travel or drive stock overland, especially over long distances. Thus *an overlander* is a drover who drives stock overland.

Oxford scholar
rs A dollar.

Oz
Australia. *Ozzie* means Australian.

Pp
Pig's arse!
Pakapoo ticket
Pavement pizza
Poke borak
Purler!
Pass the buck
Possum guts
Piss in the wind
Plon
Pull up stakes
Piss-ant around

P

pack, gone to the
In a state of deterioration, failure or total collapse.

pack death
also packing death; pack/ing the shits; pack/ing your daks; pack/ing polenta
To be very, very nervous or afraid.

pack it in
To quit or give up.

paddle pop
see **icypole**

Paddo
abbrev. Paddington (an inner suburb of Sydney).

paddock
A fenced area of land on a farm, often encompassing hundreds or thousands of hectares: e.g. 'Help me move these sheep to the top paddock.'

pakapoo ticket
hist. Something messy, muddled or difficult to decipher, especially writing. (From a Chinese lottery game, Pakapoo, that was popular on the Australian goldfields.)

pan
To criticise or condemn: e.g. 'The film was universally panned.'

panic stations, to be at
To be frenzied, chaotic or hectic.

paralytic
Exceedingly drunk, to the point of being physically incapacitated.

pash
An enthusiastic or deep kiss: e.g. 'I can't believe she pashed him, she must have been so drunk!' *Pashing* is the act of performing such a kiss.

pass in one's marble
To die.

pass over the Great Divide
To die. (The Great Dividing Range is Australia's largest mountain range and many early explorers died while trying to cross it.)

pass the buck
To palm off responsibility or blame someone else.

pav
abbrev. A pavlova (a popular meringue cake that was allegedly created by an Australian chef in honour of Russian ballerina Anna Pavlova.)

pavement pizza
Vomit.

pearler
see **purler**

peeny pointers
see **budgie smugglers**

P

perhapser
An act with uncertain consequences. (Originally a cricketing term for a risky or hazardous stroke.)

perish, to do a
To die, especially of dehydration/thirst.

perk
To vomit.

perv or **perve**
1 To watch or look at lustfully or with lewd intent: e.g. 'Have a perv at those sheilas.'
2 A person who pervs.

petrol-head
A person who is very interested in cars and, usually, also motor racing.
cf. rev-head

physio
abbrev. Physiotherapy or a physiotherapist.

piccy
abbrev. A picture or photograph: e.g. 'Show us a piccy of your new bloke.'

pick a winner in a two-horse race, couldn't
Said of a stupid or useless person.

pie floater
A meat pie served floating in a bowl of pea soup, invented as a takeaway in Adelaide (the state capital of South Australia).

pig's arse!
also pig's bum!
int. Rubbish! Nonsense! That's not true/correct!

pike
often derog. To let down, back down or retract on a promise. e.g. 'So are you coming to the party? Don't tell me you're going to pike again!' Thus a *piker* is a person who regularly pikes.

pinko
joc. A socialist, communist or anyone espousing left-wing politics.

piss
1 Urine.
2 To urinate.
3 Alcohol, especially beer. *On the piss* means to be on a drinking spree.

piss and wind, all
see **all piss and wind**

piss-ant around
To dawdle or fool about.

pissed
1 Drunk.
2 Angry or irritated.

pissed as a fart
also pissed as a newt; pissed as a parrot; pissed to the eyeballs
Very drunk.

pisser
1 A pub.
2 A penis.
3 Something really bad.
4 Something really good.
5 Something really funny.

piss in someone's pocket
To fawn over or flatter somebody.

piss in the wind
To do something badly or incompetently, or to attempt something that is unachievable.

piss on you if you were on fire, wouldn't
Said of a nasty, callous person.

pisspot
A habitual drinker or drunkard.

piss-weak
Pathetic, spineless or poorly performed: e.g. 'Your argument is piss-weak.'

PJs
Pyjamas.

plastered
Drunk.

play funny buggers
To fool around, be dishonest or try to con: e.g. 'I'm not here to play funny buggers; this deal is fair dinkum.'

play lunch
A small meal that pre-school and primary-school children eat for morning tea.

plonk
Wine, especially cheap or poor-quality wine.

pocket rocket
A penis.

poddy
An unbranded calf.

point Percy at the porcelain
(of a man) To urinate.

point the bone at
To put a hex or jinx on. (From the Aboriginal ritual of pointing a bone or stick at an enemy to harm or kill them.)

poke
1 To punch or hit.
2 To have sexual intercourse.

poke borak
To mock or tease someone.

pokies
abbrev. Poker machines, which grace Australia's huge number of gambling and social venues: e.g. 'I just got paid, so I'm off to play the pokies.'

pollie or **polly**
abbrev. A politician.

pom or **pommie** or **pommy**
often derog. A person from England. Often used in insulting combinations, such as *pommy bastard*.

Pommyland
England.

pong
A bad smell.

poo, in the
In trouble or in someone's bad books.

pooey or **poohy**
Smelly or otherwise disagreeable: e.g. 'She's in a pooey mood.'

poor as a bandicoot
Very poor.

port
abbrev. Portmanteau (a suitcase or overnight bag).

possie or **pozzie**
A position: e.g. 'We should get there early so we can find a good possie.'

possum
A pet name or term of endearment.

possum guts
A coward.

possum up a gum tree, like a
Very happy or satisfied.

potato scallop
also potato cake
A slice of potato that has been dipped in batter and then deep-fried. (Whether this fish-and-chip-shop staple is called a *potato scallop* or a *potato cake* depends on which state you are in.)

poultice
A lot of money.

pozzie
see **possie**

preggers
abbrev. Pregnant.

pressie or **prezzy**
abbrev. A present or gift.

prollie
A deliberate mispronunciation of probably.

psych oneself up
To put oneself in the right frame of mind or try to find the courage to do something: e.g. 'I really had to psych myself up before the exam.'

PT
acr. Public transport: e.g. 'Are you catching PT to the footy game tonight?'

pub
abbrev. Public house (a hotel, implicitly one that serves alcoholic beverages).

pull a swiftie or **pull a swifty**
To trick or deceive.

pull out, digger – the dogs are pissing on your swag
Get out, step down or give up. (Reportedly said in 1991 by then Foreign Minister Gareth Evans to Prime Minister Bob Hawke, to suggest it was time to stand down.)

pull someone's tit
To tease or make fun of someone.

pull up stakes
also pull up stumps
To leave or get ready to leave.

pull your finger out!
int. Hurry up! Get a move on!

pull your head in!
int. An exhortation to be quiet or mind your own business.

punt
To gamble or bet.

punter
A person who gambles or bets.

purler or **pearler**
Something outstanding or admirable: e.g. 'That performance was a purler!'

pushover
A person or thing that is very easy to do, master or acquire.

put the acid on
To put pressure on someone for a favour, especially a monetary one: e.g. 'I think it's time I put the acid on my boss about that raise.'

put the billy on
To put water on to boil.

put the bite on
also put the hard word on
To put pressure on someone for something, especially money or sex.

put the mockers on
also put the moz/mozz on
To put a curse or jinx on; to bring bad luck to.

pyjama game
A one-day cricket match. (In World Series one-day cricket, the team members wear loose-fitting, brightly coloured outfits that are deemed to resemble pyjamas.)

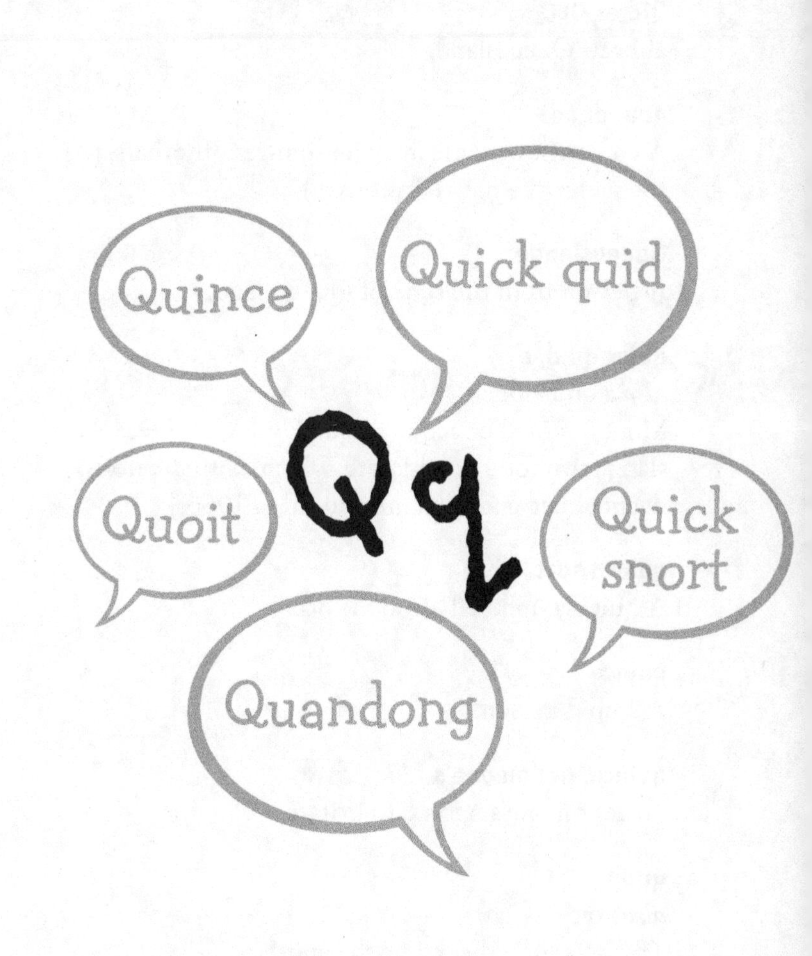
Quince
Quick quid
Qq
Quoit
Quick snort
Quandong

Q

Qld or **QLD**
abbrev. Queensland.

quandong
A con artist or someone who sponges off others. (Also the name of a native fruit tree.)

Queenslander
A person from the state of Queensland.

quick quid, a
also a quick buck
Money earned or acquired quickly. (A quid was the slang term for a pound note, which existed before decimal currency was introduced in 1966.)

quick snort
A quickly imbibed alcoholic drink.

quince
A stupid person.

quince, get on one's
To get on one's nerves; to irritate.

quoit
also coit
The bottom or backside; the anus.

Rort
Rashie
Rust-bucket
Rattle your dags!
Rafferty's rules
Rr
Rev-head
Rough as guts
Rack off!
Run like a hairy goat
Rat coffin
Rough diamond
Rego
Root rat
Rabbit on

R

rabbit on
To talk incessantly: e.g. 'Quit rabbiting on, will you!'

race off
To seduce.

race that stops a nation, the
The Melbourne Cup horserace.

rack off!
also rack off hairy legs!
int. Go away! Get lost!

Rafferty's rules
No rules at all, no holds barred; disorderly or shambolic.

ragged
Tired or unwell: e.g. 'You look pretty ragged this morning.'

raincoat
A condom.

raining palaces I'd be hit on the head by the dunny door, if it was
I never have any luck; I'm terribly unlucky.

ralph
To vomit.

rapt
see **wrapped**

rare as hens' teeth
see **scarce as hens' teeth**

rare as rocking-horse shit
see **scarce as rocking-horse shit**

rashie
A lycra top worn under a wetsuit to prevent rashes developing, or worn over bathers to give protection from the sun.

ratbag
An eccentric person or rascal, who may also be somewhat disreputable.

rat coffin
A meat pie. (A reference to the possibly dubious quality of the meat used in the average pie.)

rather pick up a death adder than a shovel
Said of a person who is exceedingly lazy or slothful.

rat-shit
1 Bad or awful: e.g. 'That hat looks rat-shit on you.'
2 Miserable or unwell: e.g. 'I feel totally rat-shit today.'
3 Broken, hopeless or useless: e.g. 'This car is rat-shit.'

rattle your dags!
int. Hurry up! Get a wriggle on! (Dags are the bits of wool around a sheep's bottom, often matted with excrement.)

R

rat up a drainpipe, like a
Very quick or fast: e.g. 'He was out of there like a rat up a drainpipe.'

raw prawn
see **don't come the raw prawn**

razoo or **rahzoo**
see **brass razoo**

razz
To mock, taunt or tease.

razzle
To steal.

reckon, I
I certainly think so; too right; absolutely.

redback
1 A red-back spider, a venomous Australian species.
2 An Australian $20 note (due to the red colour of the note).

red ned
Red wine, especially cheap red wine.

reds
Fleas.

reef or **reef off**
To steal, especially money.

Reg Grundy's
also Grundy's
rs Undies (underpants). (Reginald Grundy was a very successful Australian television entrepreneur and producer from the 1960s to the 1990s.)

rego
abbrev. Registration: e.g. 'Don't forget to renew your car rego.'

rellies
also rellos
abbrev. Relatives.

removalist
A person or company that transfers household or business furniture and other belongings from one place to another: e.g. 'I hope the removalists don't break anything this time!'

rev-head
A person who is very interested in cars and, usually, also motor racing, particularly a person who enjoys driving their own car at high speeds.
cf. petrol-head

ridgy-didge
The truth, or the genuine article.

right-oh! or **righto!** or **righty-ho!**
int. A general exclamation of agreement or acceptance.

ring
An anus.

ringer
The name for the fastest shearer in the woolshed.

ring-in
A substitute, normally last-minute and often fraudulent. (Originally used in horseracing, when a horse was fraudulently substituted for the one intended to run.)

ring one's tail
To yield, give in or reveal cowardice. A *ringtail* is a coward.

rinsed
also half-rinsed
Drunk.

ripped
Drunk.

ripper
also ripsnorter
Something wonderful or admirable: e.g. 'You little ripper!'

rissole
also rozzer
An RSL (Returned Services League of Australia) club. (RSL clubs typically serve as venues for community gatherings and activities. Nowadays they may also have an area for pokies.)

road train
A huge truck, which consists of a conventional prime mover pulling two or more trailers or semi-trailers (instead of the usual one). Most often seen in remote areas; the longest ones are legally allowed to operate only in the Northern Territory.

roar someone up
also roar the shit out of someone
To severely reprimand someone.

Rock, the
Uluru, also known as Ayers Rock, is the famous sandstone monolith situated south-west of Alice Springs in the Northern Territory.

rock-hopper
A person who fishes from rocks on the seashore.

rock up
To arrive, often without invitation or prior notice: e.g. 'We rocked up to the party about 10 o'clock.'

rollie or **roly**
A hand-rolled cigarette.

R

ron

A contraction of 'later on': e.g. 'I think I'll save one for ron.'

roo

abbrev. A kangaroo.

roo bar

also bull bar

A metal bar attached to the front of a car, truck or ute to offer protection if a kangaroo is struck while driving.

root

1 To have sexual intercourse.

2 A person with whom one has had sexual intercourse: e.g. 'He was the worst root I've ever had.'

rooted

1 Exhausted or confounded: e.g. 'I was up all night and now I'm absolutely rooted.'

2 Broken, ruined or destroyed: e.g. 'This computer is rooted.'

root rat

A promiscuous person.

ropeable or **ropable**

Very angry, often violently: e.g. 'Dad was ropeable when he found out I didn't go to school yesterday.'

rort
1 A ruse or scam.
2 A lively or wild party.

rotten
Drunk.

rough, a bit
also a bit strong; a bit rugged
Unfair, undeserved or unreasonable. 'That's a bit rough!'

rough as guts
also rough as bags; rough as a pig's breakfast; rough as goat's knees
Very rough, uncultured or wild.

rough diamond
A person who appears a bit rough or unrefined but is a nice, kind person underneath.

rough end of the pineapple, the
Unfair treatment or a difficult experience: e.g. 'My boss really gave me the rough end of the pineapple today.'

rough enough for the bush
Good enough; passable: e.g. 'The bookshelf I built isn't perfect, but it's rough enough for the bush.'

roughie
A rough or wild person or thing.

rough someone up
To fight with someone, implicitly to be the one dealing out the blows. A *rough-up* is a fight or brawl.

rough trot, a
A period of difficulty or disadvantage. 'Don't be too tough on him, he's had a rough trot.'
see also **good trot**

rouseabout
hist. A handyman or someone employed to do odd jobs on a sheep or cattle station. Nowadays, any handyman or odd-jobs man.

rouse on
To scold or berate.

rowdy
A nickname for a quiet or shy person.

royal order, the
also the order of the boot; the boot
A sacking or rejection: e.g. 'The company was cutting back, so I got the royal order.'

rubber johnny
A condom.

rubbity-dub
also rubbity
rs Pub.

rugger bugger
A person who plays or follows rugby, usually Rugby Union.

rug up
To wear warm clothes suitable for cold weather: e.g. 'You kids better get rugged up, it's freezing outside.'

run, get the
To get the sack; to be fired.

run around like a chook with its head cut off
also run around like a headless chook
To be frantic, disorganised or very busy: e.g. 'She was running around like a headless chook trying to get everything ready for the party.'

run like a hairy goat
To run badly in a race, especially in horseracing.

runner, do a
To depart or flee, usually to dodge a responsibility: e.g. 'He did a runner when he found out she was pregnant.'

run rings around someone
To outperform someone by a wide margin.

rust-bucket
Something, usually a car, which is old and in bad condition.

Sink the slipper
Strewth
Sanger
Sambie
Spit the dummy
Snag
Scarce as hen's teeth
Sheila
Stone the crows!
Snake juice
Silly as a two-bob watch
She'll be apples
Sparrow's fart
Shaggin' wagon
Sweet FA
Stubby

SA
acr. South Australia.

saltie
abbrev. A saltwater crocodile.

Salvos, the
also Sallies
abbrev. The Salvation Army (a welfare organisation).

sambie
also sambo; sanger
abbrev. A sandwich.

sandgroper
also groper
A person from Western Australia.

sandwich short of a picnic, a
also a few sandwiches short of a picnic
Said of a stupid or dim-witted person.

sanger
see **sambie**

sav
abbrev. Saveloy sausage (a type of frankfurter).

scads
A large amount; lots.

scarce as hen's teeth
also rare as hen's teeth; scarce/rare as rocking-horse shit
Very rare or in short supply.

scone
A head: e.g. 'That bald guy has a funny-shaped scone.'

scorcher
An extremely hot day: e.g. 'I saw on the telly that it's going to be a real scorcher tomorrow.'

scratchie or **scratchy**
An instant-win lottery ticket that you scratch to reveal your prize.

scrub
1 Bushland.
2 The scrub can refer to rural areas in general.

scumbag
A contemptible or abhorrent person: e.g. 'Stop lying to me, you scumbag!'

scungy or **skungy**
Dirty, grotty or grubby.

send her down, Hughie!
A plea for rain. Or conversely, an exclamation of delight when rain begins to fall. ('Hughie' was traditionally a bush-dweller's epithet for God.)

septic tank or **septic**
rs Yank (an American).

serve, give someone a
To scold or berate someone. If you *cop a serve*, you are on the receiving end.

servo
abbrev. Service station.

shag
1 To have sexual intercourse.
2 A person with whom one has had sexual intercourse.

shagged
1 Very tired or exhausted.
2 Bothered: e.g. 'I really can't be shagged going out tonight.'

shaggin' wagon
A motor vehicle, often a panel van, intended for sexual encounters.

shag on a rock, like a
Alone, lonely or miserable. (A shag is a type of ocean cormorant.)

shake hands with the wife's best friend
also shake hands with the unemployed
(of a man) To urinate.

sharpest knife in the cutlery drawer, not the
Said of a stupid or dim-witted person.

shat off, to be
To be fed up, annoyed or really angry.

sheep's back, on the
Dependent on wool production and sales. (Often used to describe the Australian economy.)

sheep station
A farm where sheep are raised for wool or meat.

sheila
often derog. A girl or woman.

shellacking
A trouncing.

she'll be apples
also she's apples; she'll be right; she'll be jake; she'll be sweet
Don't worry, everything is going to be fine.

sherbet
An alcoholic drink, especially beer: e.g. 'I'm off to the pub for a few sherbets.'

shick
also shicked; shickered
Drunk.

shicker
To drink.

shin off
To depart hurriedly.

shiralee
hist. A swag (a roll of personal belongings and bedding).

shirty
Short-tempered or grumpy.

shit a brick!
int. An exclamation of surprise, irritation or exasperation.

shit-faced
Drunk.

shithead
derog. A nasty, disliked or horrible person.

shithouse
also shouse
1 A toilet, especially one that is outdoors.
2 Very bad or terrible.

shit-kicker
also shit-shoveller
A person who performs menial, unpleasant or degrading work.

shit-load
A large amount or a lot: e.g. 'I've got a shit-load of work to get through.'

shivoo or **shivaroo**
A party or bender.

shocker, a
Something terrible, dreadful or unfashionable: e.g. 'The dress she wore was an absolute shocker.'

shonky
Of dubious quality or sincerity; unreliable or suspicious: e.g. 'He's one of those shonky secondhand-car salesmen.'

shook on
To be interested in or attracted to someone or something: e.g. 'She sure seems shook on him.'

shoot the breakers
To surf.

shoot through
To depart hurriedly and unexpectedly.

shoot through like a Bondi tram
To depart swiftly and unexpectedly. (Trams no longer run in the Sydney suburb of Bondi, but when they did they were notoriously speedy owing to the small number of stops on the beach-side part of the track.)

short arms and deep pockets
Said of someone who is miserly or stingy with money.

shouse
see **shithouse**

shout
To treat somebody by paying for their share of something; especially used in reference to buying a round of beers: e.g. 'I know you're broke, so I'll shout you lunch today.'

shove off
also sling off
1 To depart.
2 int. 'Get lost!'

show pony
A person who has good looks and presentation, but not much else.

shrapnel
Coins, particularly the smaller denominations: e.g. 'I hope you don't mind me paying with all this shrapnel.'

shyster
A criminal or conman.

sickie
Time taken off work for illness, often pretend illness.
see also **chuck a sickie**

sidekick
see **offsider**

silly as a two-bob watch
also silly as a wheel; silly as a hatful of arseholes; silly as a hatful of worms; silly as a bum full of Smarties
Very silly or stupid. (A 'two-bob watch' would be a very cheap and presumably unreliable watch.)

silly season, the
The Christmas–New Year period.

silvertail
A wealthy or upper-class person.

singing budgie, the
A nickname for pop diva Kylie Minogue.

sink a few
To drink some beers. e.g. 'We'll probably sink a few while we're watching the game.'

sink the sausage
also sink the sav
(of a man) To have sexual intercourse.

sink the slipper
To kick someone, often when they're down; used both literally and figuratively. (An Aussie variation on 'put the boot in'.)

siphon the python
see **syphon the python**

sixes and sevens, at
Confused or disordered.

six of one, half a dozen of the other
It's all the same; both options are actually equal; much of a muchness.

six-pack
A pack containing six cans or bottles of beer: e.g. 'Let's pick up a six-pack on the way to the party.'

skerrick
Very little; a scrap. Most often used in the phrase *not a skerrick*, meaning nothing or none.

skint
Penniless or out of money: e.g. 'Could you get this round? I'm skint.'

skippy
A kangaroo. (After the popular 1960s Australian television show for children, *Skippy the Bush Kangaroo*.)

skite
1 To boast or show off.
2 A braggart or show-off. (*also* skiter)

skol
1 To drink an alcoholic beverage in one go.
2 **int.** A toast or salutation, equivalent to 'cheers.'

slab
also case; block
A carton of beer, normally containing 24 cans or bottles of beer: e.g. 'Can you bring a slab to the party?'

slacker
also slack arse
A person who is lazy or shirks their obligations.

sledge
To criticise, abuse or mock. In cricket: a form of gamesmanship in which verbal abuse is used to distract and aggravate an opponent. *Sledging* is the act, and a *sledger* is one who performs such an act.

sleepout
A veranda (porch) that has been converted into an extra bedroom.

sling off at
To insult or abuse.

slops
Beer.

smart-arse
A know-it-all.

smashed
Drunk.

smell of an oily rag, on the
Using very little money or resources: e.g. 'We're living on the smell of an oily rag these days.'

smoke, in
In hiding.

smoke-oh or **smoke-o** or **smoko**
also spell-oh; spell-o; spello
A short rest or tea-break.

smokes
Cigarettes.

smoodge
1 To kiss, cuddle or caress. (*also* smooch)
2 To flatter.

snag
A sausage.

snag short of a barbie, a
also a few snags short of a barbie; a chop short of a barbie
Of lower-than-average intelligence or not completely sane.

snake juice
Any very strong alcohol.

snake's hiss
rs Piss.

snaky or **snakey**
Irritable or bad-tempered.

snoot
An unpleasant or difficult person; a snob.

snorker
A sausage.

snorter
A very hot day.

snout on, have a
To hold a grudge against someone.

soapie
A soap opera.

soda, a
Something easy to do or achieve.

soft-cock
derog. A man considered to be weak or cowardly, or to not be up to a task.

soft cop, a
also a sweet cop
A safe or easy time, task or occupation.

soft drink
Any sweet non-alcoholic carbonated drink. (The equivalent of US soda or pop, and UK fizzy drink.)

so hungry I could eat a horse and chase the jockey
also so hungry I could eat the crutch out of a low-flying duck; so hungry I could eat the arsehole out of a dead dingo; so hungry I could eat the arse out of a ragdoll
Extremely hungry.

solid
Excessive or unfair: e.g. 'That's a bit solid!'

sonky
Foolish, silly or ridiculous.

sook
A timid person, coward or cry-baby: e.g. 'Dry your tears and stop being such a sook.'

sool
To encourage to chase, tackle or attack (usually of a dog): e.g. 'They sooled their dog onto the intruder.'

southerly buster
A strong southerly wind.

souvenir
To steal.

spag
abbrev. Spaghetti.

spag bol
abbrev. Spaghetti bolognaise.

sparky or **sparkie**
An electrician.

sparrow's fart
Very early in the morning; daybreak: e.g. 'I was up at sparrow's fart to drive to the airport.'

spear, get the
To be sacked from one's job. Hence *to give someone the spear* is to give them the sack.

spear the bearded clam
(of males) To have sex with a woman.

specky or **speccy**
A spectacular mark in Australian Rules football; especially one made by leaping high into the air, often by vaulting off the back or shoulders of a teammate or opponent.

Speedos
An Australian brand of swimming costume; also used to refer to any tight-fitting men's bathers.

Speewa or **Speewah**
A mythical outback cattle station. (The place often appears in the stories and legends of Australian bushmen and farm workers.)

spell-oh
see **smoke-oh**

spew
Vomit.

spewing
Extremely angry or irritated: e.g. 'I was spewing when I found out my husband had crashed my car.'

spider
A soft drink with ice-cream added to it.

spinner
The person who tosses the coins in the gambling game of two-up.

spit the dummy
To totally lose patience and become enraged. Such an outburst is called a *dummy spit*. (A 'dummy' is a rubber teat given to a child to suck.)

spitting chips
Very angry.

splash one's boots
(of men) To urinate.

sport
A friendly term of address, similar to 'mate.'

spruiker
A person who is employed to stand in front of a shop or stall and noisily promote its wares to passers-by. By extension, any person who is haranguing others.

spuds
1 Potatoes.
2 Testicles.

spunk
also spunk rat
An attractive or sexually appealing person: e.g. 'That surfie is a total spunk.' Such a person is said to be *spunky*.

square off
To set things straight, apologise or explain when there's been a misunderstanding.

squatter
hist. A person who established a sheep or cattle farm on crown land, often without permission to do so.

squattocracy
A collective term for the well-off farming families who are thought to regard themselves as aristocracy.
see also **squatter**

squib
1 A shy or cowardly person.
2 To behave in a timid or cowardly way.
3 A fib.
4 Something planned that fails or never eventuates.

squib on, to
To deceive, dob on or betray someone.

squiz or **squizz**
A look.

stack
1 A crash or accident: e.g. 'There was a big stack on the freeway this morning.'
2 To crash or have an accident: e.g. 'I stacked my bike.'

stack on
1 To put on or perform: e.g. 'To stack on an act.'
2 To add a lot: e.g. 'Wow, he's really stacked on the weight in the last few months.'

station
A sheep or cattle farm.

steak and kidney
rs Sydney.

steam
Wine, especially cheap fortified wine.

Steel Rudds
rs Spuds (potatoes). (Steele Rudd was the pseudonym of humorist Arthur Hoey Davis, who created the popular rural characters Dad and Dave.)

sterks, to give one the
To annoy, irritate or make angry.

sticks, the
Any remote rural area.

stick out like a dog's balls, to
also to stand out like dog's ball
To be self-evident, obvious or conspicuous.

stick-up
1 A hold-up, hitch or dilemma.
2 **hist.** An armed robbery, especially of a coach; a hold-up.

sticky wicket
A bad or problematic situation or position.

stickybeak
1 A nosy person or busybody.
2 A look: e.g. 'Have a stickybeak at that guy's haircut!'

stiff
1 Short of or wanting.
2 Broke.

stiff as a crutch
Destitute, broke or very unlucky.

stiff cheddar!
int. Too bad!

stinker
1 A very hot day.
2 Anything difficult or unpleasant.

stinko
Drunk.

stirrer
A person who likes to stir up trouble.

stir the possum
To intentionally create conflict, cause trouble or upset things.

stockman
A man who works on a cattle station.

stone the crows!
also starve the lizards!; speed the wombat!
int. An exclamation of amazement, surprise or disbelief.

stonkered
1 Drunk.
2 Defeated, broken-down or exhausted.

stoush
A fight, especially a fist-fight.

straddle the barbed-wire fence
To sit on the fence; to not express an opinion either way.

strewth! or **struth!**
int. A fairly mild exclamation of annoyance, surprise or frustration. (A contraction of 'God's truth!').

strides
Trousers.

strike a light!
also strike me dead!; strike me pink/blue!; strike me lucky!
int. An exclamation of amazement or joy.

Strine
A hypothetical language spoken by Australians. It reflects the broad Australian accent and its flattened vowels and squashed syllables: e.g. 'Strine' (Australian); 'Icon ardlywait' (I can hardly wait); 'G'dye, myte' (G'day, mate); 'Egg nisher' (Air conditioner).
see also **Emma Chisit**

strong, a bit
see **rough, a bit**

strongarm
To bully or intimidate, especially through physical violence.

stubbie or **stubby**
Anything small or truncated, but especially a small (375 ml) bottle of beer. In the plural form *stubbies,* it means a pair of very brief men's shorts, which in the past were often worn by labourers and tradies.

stubbie cooler
also stubby cooler; stubbie/stubby holder
An insulated holder, usually made of neoprene, for keeping one's bottle of beer cold.

stubbie short of a six-pack, a
Said of a stupid or dim-witted person.

stuffed
1 Exhausted: e.g. 'I'm stuffed after that run.'
2 Broken or useless: e.g. 'My computer is stuffed.'
3 Bothered: e.g. 'I can't be stuffed.'

stuff up
To botch or make a mess of things. A *stuff-up* is the result of stuffing up.

stunned
Drunk.

stunned mullet, like a
To be stupid, unaware, dazed, bewildered or unmoving: e.g. 'Well don't just sit there like a stunned mullet, go and answer the door!'

subbie
abbrev. A subcontractor. (Often used in the building industry.)

sudden death on
Inclined to impose strict penalties or punishment: e.g. 'That teacher is sudden death on talking during class.'

suit, a
A person who works in an office.

sundowner
hist. /derog. An itinerant worker who typically arrived at a cattle station at, or just before, dusk – i.e. too late to do any work that day, so he would receive lodgings and a meal essentially 'for free.'

sunnies
abbrev. Sunglasses.

Sunshine State, the
Queensland.

surf and turf
A meal that includes both seafood and meat.

surfie
A person who surfs.

super

1 **abbrev.** Superannuation.
2 **abbrev.** Superphosphate.

suss

abbrev. Suspect or suspicious: e.g. 'He was acting a bit suss, don't you think?'

suss out

To investigate or check out: e.g. 'Let's go suss out the new coffee shop in town.'

swag

1 **hist.** A roll of personal belongings and bedding carried by a swagman.
2 A lot of something, especially money or prizes: e.g. 'The film won a swag of awards.'

swagman

also swaggie

hist. A wanderer or itinerant worker, who carried their belongings with them in a swag.

sweat on

To dwell on or wait anxiously for something.

sweet, she's

also she'll be sweet

Everything is okay/set/ready.

sweetener

An inducement or incentive, usually monetary.

sweet FA
Nothing or almost nothing (an abbreviation of sweet fuck all): e.g. 'I'm doing sweet FA this weekend.'

swiftie
see **pull a swiftie**

swimmers
A swimming costume.

Sydney harbour
rs A barber.

Sydney or the bush!
It's all or nothing!

Sydneysider
also Sydneyite
A person from Sydney, the state capital of New South Wales.

syphon the python
also siphon the python
(of males) To urinate.

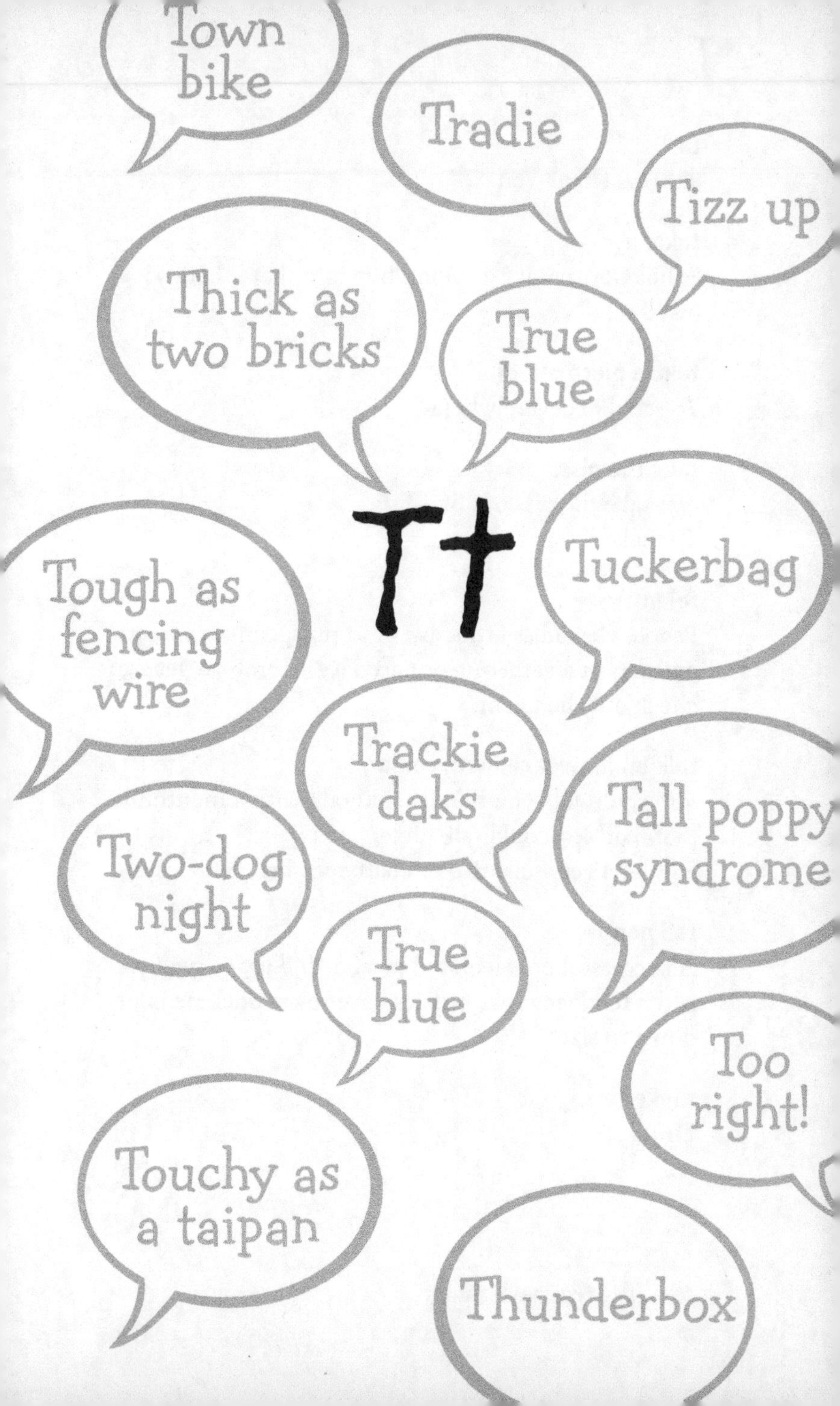
Town bike
Tradie
Tizz up
Thick as two bricks
True blue
Tt
Tough as fencing wire
Tuckerbag
Trackie daks
Tall poppy syndrome
Two-dog night
True blue
Too right!
Touchy as a taipan
Thunderbox

T

ta
abbrev. Thank you.

take, a
A hoax or fraud: e.g. 'Don't buy into that scheme, it's just a take.'

take a piece out of
To scold or severely berate.

take the piss
also take the piss out of
To make fun of or tease.

talent
People viewed as attractive or as prospective romantic partners at a gathering or party: e.g. 'Come on, let's go check out the talent.'

talk under wet cement, could
also could talk you blind; could talk with a mouthful of marbles; could talk underwater
Said of a very talkative or chatty person.

tall poppy
A successful or celebrated person. *Tall poppy syndrome* is the tendency that Aussies have to cut such people down to size.

tanked
Drunk.

Tas. or **TAS**
also Tassie; Tazzie
abbrev. Tasmania.

Taswegian
A person from the state of Tasmania.

ta-ta
Goodbye.

tea
The evening meal; dinner: e.g. 'What would you like for tea tonight?'

tear into
1 To attack or tackle in a very determined way: e.g. 'They tore into their chores.'
2 To berate or reproach somebody in an aggressive way: e.g. 'When she found out what they'd done, she really tore into them.'

technicolour yawn
also colourful yawn
Vomit.

telly
Television.

Territorian
A person from the Northern Territory.

T

thanks
1 Thank you.
2 Please: e.g. 'I'll have a Hawaiian pizza with extra pineapple, thanks.'

thick as two bricks
also thick as two (short) planks
Said of a stupid or dim-witted person.

things are crook at Tallarook
also things are crook at Muswellbrook; things are weak at Julia Creek
Things are bad. (Tallarook is a tiny country town in the state of Victoria.)

thingummyjig
also thingummybob; thingummy; thingumabob; thingo
Something you can't remember or think of a name for: e.g. 'Pass me that thingummyjig will you?'

this side of the black stump
see **black stump**

thongs
Simple rubber sandals held onto the foot by a V that passes between the first and second toes. (The equivalent of US flip-flops.)

threshing machine, fight like a
see **fight like a threshing machine**

throw a map
also throw sixes
To vomit.

throw a seven
To collapse or die.

thugby
derog. Rugby.

thunderbox
A toilet, usually outdoors.

tickets on oneself, to have
To be arrogant, vain or conceited.

tight
Miserly or stingy with money.

Tim Tam slam
also Tim Tam suck
A technique for eating a Tim Tam biscuit whereby the eater bites opposite corners off the biscuit, then sucks tea or coffee up through it and quickly eats it before it falls apart.

Tim Tam short of a packet, a
Said of a stupid or dim-witted person. (Tim Tam is a brand of chocolate biscuit immensely popular with Australians.)

tin-arse
also tin-bum
A very lucky or wealthy person.

tin ear
An eavesdropper.

tin lid
rs Kid (child).

tinnie or **tinny**
1 A can of beer. *To crack a tinnie* is to open a beer.
2 A small, open aluminium boat.

tired and emotional
Drunk.

tits on a bull, useful as
see **useful as a one-legged man in an arse-kicking competition**

tizz up
To dress up for an occasion, or beautify.

tizzy
Flashy, gaudy or overly extravagant: e.g. 'Who's she trying to impress with that tizzy outfit ?'

toey
Impatient, irritable, anxious or expectant.

togs
A swimming costume.

tonguing for a beer
Really thirsty and ready for a beer.

tonk
A foolish or stupid person.

tonked, get
To be hit or beaten in a fight.

too right!
int. You bet! That's true!

Toorak tractor
derog. A four-wheel drive (off-road vehicle) owned by a city dweller and mostly (or only) driven in the suburbs. (Toorak is a wealthy suburb of Melbourne.) *cf.* North Shore tank

top drop
Good wine.

Top End, the
The far north of the Northern Territory, around Darwin. Someone from this area is called a *Top-ender*.

touchy as a taipan
Said of someone who is very irritable, hot-tempered or moody.

tough as fencing wire
Very tough.

town bike, the
A woman who is thought to be sexually promiscuous.

trackie
abbrev. A tracksuit (known in the US as a sweatsuit).

trackie daks
also trackies
Tracksuit pants.

tradie
abbrev. A tradesperson.

triantelope
A huntsman spider. (A large and hairy Australian spider often mistakenly called a tarantula.)

trimmer
An excellent or admirable person or thing: e.g. 'My new car's a real little trimmer!'

trolley dolly
An air hostess.

troppo, go
To go crazy (theoretically as the result of excessive tropical heat).

trots, the
1 Horse trotting or harness racing: e.g. 'We're off to the trots tonight.'
2 Diarrhoea: e.g. 'I've got the trots.'

trouble and strife
rs/joc. Wife.

truckie
abbrev. A truck driver; especially a long-distance truck driver.

true blue
Genuine, true or truthful.

true dinks
True or accurate: e.g. 'Is that true dinks?' ('Dinks' is a diminutive of dinkum.)

trugo
A sport invented in the 1920s by railway workers in the western suburbs of Melbourne. Players score points by using a mallet to strike a rubber wheel though the goal posts.

tube
1 A can of beer.
2 A television: e.g. 'What's on the tube?'
see also **down the tube**

tuckbag
A lunch bought from the tuckshop (school canteen), usually provided in a paper bag.

tucker
Food: e.g. 'That restaurant serves good tucker.'

tuckerbag
hist. A bag used by a swagman for carrying food.

tuckerbox
A lunchbox.

tuckered out
Tired or worn out: e.g. 'By the end of the day the kids were all tuckered out.'

tuckshop
A school canteen.

turd polishing
A futile attempt to turn something that is blatantly substandard or of terrible quality into something satisfactory or valuable.

turf out
To throw out or expel: e.g. 'I can't believe they turfed us out of the pub!'

turn
A party: e.g. 'There's a big turn on at my mate's place tonight.'

turps
Inexpensive, strong alcohol.

two bob
hist. Two shillings. Nowadays it means any small amount of money: e.g. 'Her promise isn't worth two bob' (her promise is substandard, useless or worthless); 'I put two bob each way' (I hedged my bets).
see also **silly as a two-bob watch**

two-dog night
A very cold night. (Implying that the night is so cold one would need two dogs on the bed to keep warm.)

two-pot screamer
also one-pot screamer
A person who gets drunk on very little alcohol. (A 'pot' is a measurement of alcohol, usually beer, used in some Australian states.)

two-up
A traditional Australian gambling game in which two coins are tossed into the air, and the players bet on whether they will land heads or tails.

Up your jumper!
Under-ground mutton
Up there, Cazaly!
Up the duff
Uu
Ugg boots
Up country
Up a gum tree
Ute
Undies

U

uey or **uie** or **yewie**
A U-turn.

ugg boots
also ugh boots; ug boots
Boots made from sheepskin, with the fleece retained on the inside. Often worn indoors during cold weather.

ugly as a hatful of arseholes
Said of someone who is very ugly.

Uluru
The famous rock formation in the Northern Territory, also known as Ayers Rock (Uluru is the Aboriginal name for the monolith).

umpie
abbrev. Umpire.

unco
1 abbrev. Uncoordinated.
2 An uncoordinated or clumsy person: e.g. 'Have you seen him try to play sport? He's such an unco!'

underdaks
Underpants.

underground mutton
A rabbit.

undies
abbrev. Underpants.

uni
abbrev. University.

unit
One of a number of individually owned, detached or semi-detached residences on shared land; an apartment.

up against one's duckhouse
An expression describing a setback or stumbling block in one's plans.

up a gum tree
1 Puzzled, bewildered, lost or off the track.
2 In a jam or quandary: e.g. 'Oh dear, you're really up a gum tree there.'

up and down like a bride's nightie
Erratic or fluctuating.

up country
Inland Australia or the outback.

up oneself
Conceited, stuck-up or arrogant: e.g. 'Her new boyfriend is always going on about his wonderful job. He's so up himself.'

up shit creek without a paddle
In trouble or facing a dilemma.

up the . . . (Bombers/Swans/Eagles/Pies, etc.)!
int. Come on! A spectator's shout of encouragement to their Australian Rules football team.

up the duff
Pregnant.

up there, Cazaly!
int. A shout of encouragement. (Roy Cazaly was an Aussie Rules footballer of the 1920s famed for his high marks.)

up the spout
also up the chute or up the pole
1 Useless or beyond repair: e.g. 'My computer's up the spout.'
2 Confused or confusing: e.g. 'Your argument is completely up the spout.'

up to putty
also up to mud or up to tripe
Unimportant, worthless or broken.

up your jumper!
also up you/yours for the rent!
int. A defiant or derisive retort.

us
Me: e.g. 'Can you give us a hand with this?'

useful as a glass door on a dunny
derog. Said of someone or something that is useless or hopeless.

useful as a one-legged man in an arse-kicking competition
also useful as tits on a bull; useful as an ashtray on a motorbike
derog. Said of a useless or incompetent person.

ute
abbrev. A utility vehicle. (The equivalent of a US pickup truck. These versatile work vehicles are often driven by tradesmen and farmers, as well as just about everyone else who lives in the bush.)

VB
Veg out
Vv
Vinnies
Vino
Veggies

VB
acr. Victoria Bitter (a popular Australian brand of beer).

vegies or **veggies**
abbrev. Vegetables.

veg out
To relax or hang out, often doing nothing much or watching television. (Veg is short for 'vegetate'.)

Vic. or **VIC**
abbrev. Victoria.

Victor Bravo
Victoria Bitter beer (VB).

Vinnies or **Saint Vinnies**
abbrev. St Vincent de Paul (a welfare organisation).

vino
Inexpensive wine, usually of poor quality.

Wag
Well under
Westie
Wake up, Australia!
Wacker
Wedgie
Woop woop
Ww
Wuss
Who's robbing this coach!
Walloper
Whinge
Whip the cat
Work like a drover's dog
What's the go?
Wombat

W

WA
acr. Western Australia.

WACA
acr. The Western Australian Cricket Association cricket ground.

wacker or **whacker**
A term for a foolish or amusing person, usually used in a friendly or affectionate manner.

wag
To skip a class or a day of school or work and provide a spurious excuse, or no excuse at all: e.g. 'I hate maths, let's wag it today.'

wake up, Australia!
int. Stop daydreaming and pay attention!

walkabout, go
1 To roam or drift around the country, normally the outback; to travel nomadically.
2 To wander off or disappear for an unspecified amount of time. An item that has *gone walkabout* has been lost or misplaced.

walloper
A police officer.

Wally
A silly or foolish man: e.g. 'Don't be such a Wally.'

warb
1 A poorly paid labourer.
2 A filthy or messy person.
3 A stupid or foolish person.

warby, to feel
To feel unwell or apprehensive.

warm the set and cool the tinnies!
An expression indicating readiness for a long session of beer drinking and watching sport on television.

warwicks
rs Arms. (Short for 'Warwick Farm', a racecourse in Sydney.)

watering hole
also waterhole
A place where one buys alcoholic beverages, such as a pub: e.g. 'I think I'll nip down to the local watering hole.'

wax borer
A person who talks incessantly or boringly.

weak as piss
Weak or without strength: e.g. 'This beer is weak as piss.'

wear the green and gold
To represent Australia in an international sporting event. (Green and gold have traditionally been the colours of Australia's sporting uniforms for international competitions.)

wedding tackle
The male genitals.

wedgie
1 A wedge-tailed eagle.
2 To have one's underwear creep up between the buttocks: e.g. 'These knickers give me the worst wedgie'. *To give someone a wedgie* means to forcibly pull his/her underwear or trousers up between the buttocks.

weekender
A holiday house or beach house where weekends are spent.

weigh into
To attack or tackle energetically.

well oiled
Drunk.

well under
Very drunk: e.g. 'He was well under when we got home last night.'

westie

derog. A person who comes from the western suburbs of Sydney or Melbourne; traditionally underprivileged or of a lower socio-economic status.

Westralia

Western Australia.

wet, get

To get angry.

wet, the

also the big wet

The rainy season in Australia's central and northern regions, generally considered to be from November to April. (As opposed to the dry.)

wharfie

A person who works on the wharfs, usually as a labourer.

what's the go?

What's the plan? What's going on?

what's your game?

What are you playing at? What are you plotting? What's your motivation?

whinge

To whine, grumble or complain. A *whinger* is someone who whinges frequently or incessantly.

whip the cat
To get upset over trivial matters (as in 'to cry over spilt milk').

whistle-blower
A person who reports someone else's misbehaviour, or tells tales on a person; similar to a dobber.

white-ant
To encroach on someone else's territory; or to weaken, undermine or destabilise from within.

white lady
1 Methylated spirits (when imbibed as an alcoholic beverage).
2 Cocaine.

white maggot
derog. A term used by Aussie Rules football fans to describe the umpire.

whole box and dice, the
Everything; the lot. (An Aussie variant of 'the whole kit and caboodle'.)

who's robbing this coach!
int. Mind your own business! Keep your nose out of it!

why keep a dog and bark yourself?
Pointing out an unnecessary duplication of roles.

wigwam for a goose's bridle, it's a
A response used to answer a question when one doesn't know the actual answer, or doesn't want to give it.

willy, throw a
also chuck a willy
To lose one's temper or throw a tantrum.

willy-willy
A mini cyclone or spiralling desert dust storm.

Windies, the
The West Indian cricket team.

windy it'd blow a blue dog off its chain, so
see **blow a blue dog off its chain**

wipe-off, give the
To shun or dismiss: e.g. 'He gave me the wipe-off once he got rich.'

within cooee
see **cooee**

within a bull's roar
Nearby. *Not within a bull's roar* means very far away or not close at hand.

wog
An infection or germ, especially a bad cold or the flu.

wombat
A somewhat affectionate name for a person who is dim-witted or slow on their feet. (After the lumbering Australian marsupial of that name.)

won't have a bar of
Won't tolerate or accept: e.g. 'I tried to explain but she wouldn't have a bar of it.'

wood on, have the
To have the upper hand, or have an advantage over.

Woolloomooloo uppercut.
A kick to the testicles.

woolshed
A shed on a sheep station where the sheep are sheared.

woop woop
Any remote, far-away or alien place; a mythical outback town: e.g. 'I'm not sure exactly where they live, but it's out woop woop.'

woozy
Drunk.

work in an iron lung, wouldn't
Said of a person who is extremely lazy. (Australian entertainer Barry Humphries once said this of the Poms.)

work like a drover's dog
To work very hard, often for poor pay.

worth a cracker, not
see **cracker**

wouldn't touch it with a forty-foot pole
I wouldn't go anywhere near it; I wouldn't get involved.

wowser
also blue-nosed wowser
A puritanical person or killjoy, especially one who disapproves of drinking, gambling and other popular Aussie pursuits.

wrap or **rap**
An endorsement: e.g. 'The film got a good/bad wrap from the critics.'

wrapped or **rapt**
Pleased or very enthusiastic: e.g. 'I was wrapped when he told me he'd bought the tickets.'

wrinklies
Elderly people, often one's parents.

wuss
A weakling, whinger or coward.

yeah... nah
You little beauty!
Yobbo
Youse
XXXX
Ziff
XxYyZz
Yikes
You're not wrong!
Yankee shout
Yabbie
Zonked
Yakka
Yodel

XXXX
A brand of beer popular in Queensland (pronounced 'four ex').

yabber
To babble, rant or chatter incessantly: e.g. 'Stop yabbering, will you?'

yabbie
also lobbie
Any native freshwater crayfish. *Yabbying* is the act of catching yabbies.

yakka or **yacka**
Work or effort, especially physical labour (from an Aboriginal word). Often *hard yakka*. (Hard Yakka is also a brand of hardy workwear.)

Yank
An American.

Yankeeland
America.

Yankee shout
A round of drinks in which each person pays for themself.

Yank tank
A large, American-designed car, especially an ostentatious one.

yarra
Mad or crazy.

yeah . . . nah
int. This confusing expression can mean yes or no, depending on the context.

yewie
see **uey**

yike
A dispute, argument or brawl.

yikes!
int. An exclamation of astonishment or alarm.

yippee beans
1 Baked beans.
2 Tablets containing a stimulant such as amphetamine.

yobbo or **yob**
A ruffian, hoodlum, uncouth person or bogan.

yodel
To vomit.

you little beauty!
int. An exclamation of joy or victory.

you're not wrong!
int. I completely agree! You're so right!

you're right!
int. No problem; it's ok. (Often used in response to an apology.)

youse
You (plural: i.e. used when addressing more than one person): e.g. 'Hey guys, what are youse doing later?'

you wouldn't read about it!
int. An expression of surprise or disbelief.

yowie
A mythical animal or human-like creature said to lurk in the Australian bush; similar to a bunyip (from an Aboriginal word).

zac, not worth a
also not worth a zack
Not worth anything. (Zac was a name for a sixpenny coin in the days before decimal currency.)

ziff
A beard.

zizz
A snooze or short sleep.

zonked
Very tired, worn out or sleepy.